Good Years for the Buzzards

GOOD YEARS
=FOR THE=
BUZZARDS
JOHN DUNCKLEE

The University of Arizona Press

Tucson & London

The University of Arizona Press
Copyright © 1994
The Arizona Board of Regents
All rights reserved

⊗ This book is printed on acid-free, archival-quality paper.
Manufactured in the United States of America

99   98   97   96   95   94   6   5   4   3   2   1

Library of Congress Cataloging-in-Publication Data

Duncklee, John, 1929–
Good years for the buzzards / John Duncklee.
p.   cm.
Includes index.
ISBN 0-8165-1454-2 (acid-free paper)
1. Duncklee, John, 1929–   .   2. Ranch life—Arizona.
3. Ranchers—Arizona—Biography.   I. Title.
SF194.2.D85A3   1994
636.2′13′092—dc20   94-2451
[B]   CIP

British Cataloguing-in-Publication Data
A catalogue record for this book is available from the British
Library.

To Penny, my loving and gracious wife

Contents

the
O Bar J
Ranch

TO SASABE ROAD and THREE POINTS

Cholla Tank

Rova Tank

O BAR J HQ.

TO GUNSIGHT RANCH

HOLDING PASTURE

NORTH PASTURE

TO SCHMEIDING RANCH

TO ANVIL RANCH HQ.

Pozo Hondo

PIPELINE

Hall Tank

Middle Tank

SOUTH PASTURE

PIPELINE

TO SASABE ROAD

Copper Grantz Mine

Black Dike Mine

Pacheco Tank and Well

Yellow Bird Mine

MARANA

Avra Valley

Santa Cruz

TUCSON

THREE POINTS

Coyote Mtns.

O BAR J RANCH

Sierrita Mtns.

Altar Valley

Brawley Wash

Baboquivari Mtns.

River

San Ignacio de la Canoa Grant

Santa Rita Mtns.

Santa Cruz River

CASABE

TUBAC

Tumacacori Nat. Mon.

ARIZONA
MEXICO

NOGALES

KEY

RANCH BOUNDARY FENCE

INTERIOR FENCE

ROAD

Map by Michael Taylor

Preface

Drought has been one of the greatest challenges facing cattlemen in the Southwest since cattle were introduced by the
Spaniards. The drought of the 1950s was one of the most
persistent, if not the severest, drought in the past four hundred years.

The disappearance of entire societies, such as the Ana-
sazi, has been linked to a severe and prolonged drought in the
Southwest, and some students of drought history have theo-
ries that the drought during the Civil War may have influenced
that war's outcome. The drought during the early 1890s in the
Southwest caused the loss of at least 50 percent and by some
estimates as high as 75 percent of the cattle on the ranges.
The highest losses were in 1893. After that drought ended,
low calf crops resulted from the loss of so many bulls. Drought
returned in 1899, and by 1902 the economic losses were
heavy. During the dry years between 1916 and 1921, many
cattlemen drove their herds far into Sonora, Mexico, where
grass was more plentiful. The 1933–34 drought in the Great

Plains and the West caused the Dust Bowl and affected two-thirds of the nation. Arizona was declared a drought state.

The drought of the fifties affected the entire southern tier of states and northern Mexico. In some parts of New Mexico the dry conditions caused the death of pine trees in substantial numbers. In the Pinacate area in Arizona, west of the Altar Valley, mesquite and creosote bush suffered "drought kill." As severe as the fifties drought was in terms of rainfall, the loss of cattle never approached that of the early 1890s, because the ability to drill deep wells for permanent stock water had evolved, and livestock transportation, other than herding, made it possible to ship cattle to market or to areas not affected by the drought. In 1993 I asked a cowman who had experienced the drought of the fifties what is the greatest enemy he has to face in the cattle business. He said that it used to be drought, but he could adjust to those conditions. Now it was government regulations that bothered him most.

The cattle business is always subject to the vagaries of nature and often to the notions of society. When drought looms, the price of beef on the hoof always drops drastically; nobody wants to buy cattle during a drought. Even urban economies have been affected by severe drought, but the heavy migration into the Southwest during and after World War II caused an economic boom in the cities, so the drought that affected the livestock business had little effect on cities like Tucson and Phoenix. City dwellers are apt to worry about drought only when they open a water faucet and nothing comes out. Drought has always been a difficult word to define.

When I was confronted by the reality of the drought in 1956, I was forced to decide whether to fight for survival or quit and take my losses. I decided to fight it out. Had I known how long the drought was going to last, I might have decided differently. The O Bar J Ranch had two deep wells down to a thousand feet and one shallow, hand-dug sixty-foot well.

Without the two deep wells I could not have kept my herd of cattle. Burning the spines off cholla cactus to provide forage, as I did for so many months, would not have made any difference. Even as the drought broke in the fall of 1958 and into the spring of 1959, I couldn't help but wonder what the following summer might bring. I didn't learn about the severity ranking of the fifties drought until long after I had sold the herd.

I wish to thank Julio Betancourt, Robert Webb, Raymond Turner, and Tom Sweatnam for helpful suggestions and information. My children and friends also encouraged me to tell this story. And heartfelt thanks go to my wife, Penny, for her encouraging support and artful critiques.

Finally, I should note that I have changed the names of some of the individuals discussed in the book.

Good Years for the Buzzards

"They're Your Cows Now, John"

I had wanted to be a cowboy since the day my father took me to the rodeo at Madison Square Garden and I discovered that cowboys wore more under their chaps than their bare bottoms. In Larchmont, New York, however, there was no opportunity to learn the art of cowboying, so for a few years I had to be content with books by Will James and my own fantasies.

I was ten years old in 1939 and was spending the summer at a boy's camp in Maine when my father arrived to tell me that my mother was dead. I wasn't allowed to mourn; by the time my father broke the news to me, my mother had already been buried. I remained at the camp through the summer. My father remarried within a year, and it was impossible for me to accept my new mother. I was twelve when I was sent to Tucson to one of the private ranch schools that flourished during the forties. Each boy had his own horse, and the curriculum included Latin. I was more interested in helping the neighboring ranchers than applying myself scholastically, and without a literal translation of Caesar's *Gallic Wars* I doubt that I would have made it through the ninth grade. After three years the school ran out of grades for me and I was sent to Vermont Academy, a New England prep school. "Leaping Larry" Leavitt, the headmaster, had been a Dartmouth fullback and was successful in sending Vermont Academy graduates to his college alma mater.

My father had grown up in New Hampshire. He had never attended high school but had prospered as a corporate executive with the Frank G. Shattuck Company, a New York restaurant chain. Dartmouth became his dream for me. Vermont Academy provided good experience when I look back on it, but while I was there I felt incarcerated and longed to be back in Arizona. During my senior year I was given a copy of *The Compleat Rancher,* by Russell Bennett. After spending untold hours practically memorizing Bennett's descriptions, I wrote to him through the publisher to inquire about a job on his ranch. Bennett promptly and enthusiastically replied with an offer to hire me. The ranch turned out to be located in Alberta, Canada.

My six years at private boarding schools had made me very independent, some might even say rebellious, so after the commencement program ended, my father said, "I'll get you a job with the company this summer, and you can commute with me. Then you can go to Dartmouth in the fall."

"I already have a job, Dad," I replied.

"What doing?"

"Cowboying."

"Where?"

"Alberta, Canada."

"Where the hell is Alberta, Canada?"

"Just north of Montana."

"When are you leaving?"

"Tomorrow."

There was a long period of silence while my father pondered what to say next. "Well, suit yourself," he said finally. "You can come back and go to Dartmouth in the fall."

"I didn't apply to Dartmouth, Dad."

"What the hell are you going to do, be a goddamn cowboy all your life?"

"I might be, but I applied to the University of Arizona in Tucson, and if I get accepted, I plan to pay my own way." I headed west the next day.

It was soon obvious that cowboying was a broad term in Alberta. I spent as many hours on the bumpy seat of a hayrake behind a team of workhorses as I did in the saddle. One evening after I had unharnessed my team and seen to their feed and water, the boss came into the barn with a letter addressed to me. I had been accepted by the University of Arizona.

For the next four years I studied agriculture, took care of the horses at the ranch school I had once attended, and spent summers working on ranches in Wyoming. The Korean War interrupted college and cowboying, but after four years in the navy I returned to Tucson and finished my degree. Then I learned that Joe Miller wanted to lease his ranch. Eager, a bit foolish, but enthusiastic, I plunged into the cow business in the middle of a drought. It was not just any drought; it was on its way to becoming the most severe drought in southern Arizona in four hundred years.

I sat at the table in the kitchen of the O Bar J Ranch headquarters with Joe Miller, figuring up the tally sheet on the herd of cattle I was buying with a loan from my father. I had leased Joe's ranch of fourteen sections—that is, fourteen square miles—southwest of Tucson on the western slope of the Sierrita Mountains, and I was buying his cattle. Joe handed me his figures, and I matched them against mine to make sure he wasn't trying to teach a green kid a lesson from the beginning. In fact, it wasn't long after that that I came to realize, much to my dismay, that Joe Miller did in fact have a sharp pencil and a gift for making things go his way when it came to money. But the figures looked all right. I even checked them again to make sure that in my nervousness I hadn't counted anything twice. The reheated morning coffee was bitter, but sipping it gave me something to do while I pondered the totals for the cows, calves, bulls, and yearlings we had finished tallying that windy March afternoon in 1956. Our totals agreed, and I wrote the check.

Without further ceremony than a brief handshake, he stood up to leave. As he squeezed behind the wheel of his Cadillac he said, "They're your cows now, John," and drove away down the dusty ranch road.

I stood in the barnyard with a mixture of thoughts and emotions. I was elated that I was in the cattle business, but the suddenness of it all seemed ominous. What would I do now? From my vantage point at headquarters I looked westward down the long slope of the western Sierritas and across the Altar Valley to the beautiful chain of mountains formed, north to south, by the Coyotes, Quinlans, and Baboquivaris— the western boundary of the valley. The ranch headquarters was on a *bajada,* an alluvial fan produced by the erosion of higher elevations. I looked at the great variety of southern desert shrub covering the old, well-developed bajada of the Sierritas. Foothill palo verde seemed to dominate because of its height, but the cholla (pronounced "choya") was definitely prolific. The mesquite around the headquarters mostly bordered the arroyos in a mixture with catclaw, white thorn, and Jerusalem thorn. An occasional hackberry bush showed its dark green leaves. Beneath the shrubs there was prickly pear, burroweed, snakeweed, and scattered grasses.

Turning north, I could see into the Avra Valley, and far in the distance to the northeast the mountains west of Tucson showed through the afternoon haze. To the east, Samaniego Peak in the Sierritas drew my attention, and as I looked south I saw rugged hills studded with brush, and Stevens Mountain jutting up to interrupt the bajada. Little did I realize on that windy day in March how often over the next three years I would look in that southern direction to see if there was any chance of rain.

The Sierrita Mountains are some of the oldest in southern Arizona, and their alluvial soil is deep. Historically, water has been scarce, which has limited their use for agriculture or grazing until modern well-drilling and pumping technology improved the situation. Early Spanish efforts to use the valley for grazing were thwarted not only by the lack of year-round water for livestock but also by the constant threat of Apache raiders. Nevertheless, some Spaniards tried to engage in livestock raising. The nearest Spanish land grant, the San Ignacio de la Canoa grant, was located east and south of the Sierrita Mountains. It had originally been granted to the Ortiz brothers in 1821 and included an area of four *sitios,* more than 17,000 acres. Frederick Maish and Thomas Driscoll purchased the Canoa Ranch from the Ortiz heirs in 1876, and they rapidly increased their holdings of land and cattle.

In 1912, Levi Manning purchased all the Canoa landholdings from Maish and Driscoll for $165,000 and further increased the Canoa to 100,000 acres by acquiring some adjacent parcels. Manning named his ranch Hacienda de la Canoa. By 1921, Levi's son Howell had taken over the operation of Hacienda de la Canoa. Howell seems to have gone on a buying spree, increasing the Canoa to 400 square miles. It now stretched from the Santa Rita Mountains to Brown Canyon in the Baboquivaris and included the Palo Alto Ranch, south of the O Bar J, and the Navarro Ranch, which cornered with the O Bar J on its northeast extreme. Howell once told his son-in-law, Bill Schnaufer, that at one time the Canoa carried thirty-five to forty cowboys on the payroll and branded thirty to forty thousand head of calves a year. If 65 percent of the cows calved each year, the Hacienda de la Canoa was running twenty head of cattle to the section. According to modern range management practices, that number would be crowding the carrying capacity. Many of these Canoa cattle were probably grazing on the western slope of the Sierritas when stock water was available. Howell Manning also said that Levi and he would take inspection trips to the Palo Alto Ranch and would gather wood for cooking fires on the way because there weren't enough trees on the ranch to provide firewood. John King of the neighboring Anvil Ranch told me about using cow dung for branding fires on roundups when he was a young man helping his father, Manuel.

The Desert Homestead Act of 1916 opened the area to 640-acre homesteads, and as a result, deeded or patented sections came to be scattered throughout the valley (the north pasture of the O Bar J was a block of seven deeded sections). Most of the homesteaders, however, found that a 640-acre section in the Altar Valley was not sufficient to support a livestock enterprise, and they often severely overgrazed their land. A few, like Manuel King, acquired enough adjacent or nearby land by purchasing deeded homesteads to form a basis for leasing state and federal land for grazing. The Taylor Grazing Act, which provided leases on federal land, was passed in 1934, but only scattered parcels on the western slope of the Sierritas came under the act.

Although I had been through the curriculum of the College of Agriculture at the university, when I found myself confronted with the challenge of the drought of the fifties, I didn't realize its full significance—how it would affect not only my own life but also the vegetation patterns and even the entire cattle business in the Southwest.

Drought is part of the Southwest. In normal years in southern Arizona, there are two dry periods between the two rainy seasons. The summer storms begin in July and extend through September. They emanate from warm, moist air masses brought in from the south by an annual monsoon wind system. Heat from the ground surface causes these air masses to rise quickly, cool, and condense into rainfall. The winter rainy season is part of the cyclonic frontal systems that travel from the Pacific eastward across North America between November and March. This leaves two annual periods of little or no precipitation, but it is the extended drought periods that raise hell with the cow business. The drought of the fifties was one of these. Officially it lasted from August 1953 through April 1957—forty-five consecutive months—but there was little relief on the O Bar J until the late summer of 1958.

"They're your cows now, John." Joe Miller's words ground into my mind. I walked out to the corral and watched my three saddle horses occasionally nipping at each other in spite of a full feed bunk. I sat down on the edge of the water trough, thinking about Joe's words. Nothing seemed to drive away the empty feeling in my stomach, so I stood up, left the horses to their hay, and got into the Jeep. I decided to drive to the Pozo Hondo, which, as the name implies, was a deep well in the ranch's south pasture. I had no idea why; I just had to do something, and driving to the Pozo Hondo seemed as good a thing to do as any.

The Jeep jolted over the bumpy road and slithered through the frequent sand washes on the Sierrita bajada. Joe Miller's words still haunted me. I kept saying to myself that I had everything that I needed to make my first venture into the cow business a success. All I had to do was to work hard every day and things would turn out fine. By the time I had driven the three miles to the well, however, I had concluded that I could get up early every morning, work like hell all day and half the night, and if it didn't rain there wasn't a damn thing I could do about it. I filled the gas tank on the one-cylinder motor and started it. By the time that I had returned to headquarters I had put most of my bothers into perspective, and the situation seemed far less ominous.

The O Bar J

Every cowman and cowboy in the Altar Valley knew Joe Miller's ranch as the O Bar J, but when Joe bought the outfit he changed the name to M Flying M and registered his new brand with the Arizona Livestock Sanitary Board. The "Flying" part was the result of his air force career. It also became the source of many a chuckle among the neighbors. It looked like a mustache above the M, so Joe Miller's brand and his ranch were referred to as the Flying Mustache. I had bought both brands along with the cattle, but I branded with the O Bar J irons exclusively. I also changed the name of the ranch back to the O Bar J.

The O Bar J rangeland was abused—too many cattle for too many years, not an uncommon situation in the world. Most of the land in the fourteen sections was desert. There may have been three or at the very most four sections of desert grassland, which is definitely seasonal and is as unpredictable as the rainfall. The north pasture's seven sections of deeded land had one of the densest stands of cholla I have

9

ever seen. There were also numerous stands of palo verde, and mesquite along the arroyos. The grass was mainly six-weeks grama, so named for its longevity. It is a low-growing annual without much value as forage except when green. Two noxious plants grew prolifically: burroweed and snakeweed. Both are signs of a deteriorating range, according to range management textbooks, and they were crowding what grass there was here and in the south pasture as well.

The south pasture was at a higher elevation than the neighboring north pasture. It received more rainfall, and the composition of grasses there was more varied and of better quality for forage, but it had seen better days. The Pacheco pasture, named after the original homesteader, contained the best forage on the entire ranch. Indeed, without the perennial grasses and *guajilla*—a nutritious, low-growing bush—in the Pacheco pasture's two sections, the good years for the buzzards might have had a different ending. There was one other section next to the ranch headquarters called the Horse Pasture. It too had seen hard use over the years.

Joe Miller was not a cowman, but he thought he was. He gave me the details of the rotation system he had used, which was based on something he had read. He was convinced that his system would increase the carrying capacity of the ranch, that is, how many cattle the ranch could support. In many areas of the West, carrying capacity is given as the number of acres it takes to support one cow and her calf. In the desert Southwest, carrying capacity is more likely expressed as how many cattle can be supported per one-square-mile section. The major problem with Joe Miller's rotation system was that it assumed that the O Bar J was one homogeneous vegetation type, and he would move his cattle according to his own schedule rather than one based on the seasonality of the forage over the terrain of the ranch.

Joe Miller was keen on systems, probably because of the

time he spent as an air force colonel, or perhaps he rose to the rank of colonel because of the time he spent on his systems. Under Miller's ownership the O Bar J was a system of systems, none of which were in the best interests of the cows, or for that matter of his ranch hand, Charlie Moss.

Charlie had been a cowboy all his life, and he was a good one. I inherited Charlie when I leased the ranch. In fact, according to the lease agreement with Miller, I had to agree to keep him on for at least six months. Joe's reason for specifying this was his fear that I would default on the lease and he would be stuck with the ranch and herd with nobody to take care of the operation. For my part, the two hundred dollars a month I was paying Charlie was not unreasonable, and I was glad to have someone around who knew the herd and the ranch. I learned a lot about the ranch, the cattle, and Joe Miller from Charlie Moss in a very short period of time. Charlie was mad as hell at Miller for a variety of good reasons.

I discovered that Miller had not informed Charlie that I had leased the ranch and bought the cattle until the day before we started the roundup. Charlie also told me about Joe Miller's "incentive bonus system," which he had dangled in front of Charlie for the four years he had managed the ranch. Charlie was to receive a percentage of the net profit each year, but with Joe Miller's sharp pencil and his intention of using the ranch operation for a tax write-off, Charlie never saw a bonus the entire time he worked for Joe. Charlie could see that Miller's system of systems was running up the ranch expenses and therefore costing him his bonus. Registered breeding operations identify individual cattle by tattooing numbers inside their ears and installing ear tags made of metal for quicker identification. All this is done when a calf is branded, which adds time to the entire procedure but which is necessary to record the bloodline of the individual cattle. Commercial cattle operations have no need for such records because they are not in the business of selling breeding stock, but Joe Miller tattooed every calf that was branded on the Flying Mustache, for two reasons. Every animal was insured, so if a cow or calf died, he obtained proof for the insurance company by cutting off the tattooed ear. He also had proof to show the IRS should the occasion arise. The major problem with this system was the extra time and chousing, or chasing, it took to inspect the calf's ears at shipping time, which caused greater shrinkage, or loss of weight, when the calves were weighed. Charlie believed that ear tagging helped to kill his chance of getting a bonus, but little did he realize that Joe Miller was also writing off dinners at the Old Pueblo Club and everything else he could think of on the ranch books.

At one point Charlie had recommended to Joe that the cows needed some quality bulls if they were ever going to produce quality calves, and he was happy when Joe went to New Mexico to buy eight bulls from a world-renowned Hereford breeder. However, when the bulls walked off the truck and down the loading chute of the headquarters corrals, Charlie's happiness faded quickly. It was obvious that the "reputation breeder" had taken the opportunity to unload a bunch of poor-quality bulls on Miller, who was no judge of cattle. Charlie summarized his feelings toward the New Mexico bulls by saying, "These cracker-assed sons of bitches wouldn't even make a good pen of steers. This is the only outfit I ever worked for where the cows outweigh the bulls."

The ten-year lease between Joe Miller and me was another example of one of Joe's systems. It was so complicated that my attorney charged me three hundred dollars to read it and tell me what I was getting myself into. The monthly lease payments were based on the average price of weaner calves reported at the Los Angeles Stockyards for a six-month period, so every six months we were to reevaluate the monthly payment. I also held an option to purchase the ranch based on the same system. For the first six months the payment was $265, less than a dollar per head per month, which was certainly reasonable. Fortunately or unfortunately, the system fell apart about a year later when the Los Angeles cattle market closed permanently.

The day after the tally was finished, I began hearing it all from Charlie and how cheated he felt. His tirade against Miller set me to wondering just what kind of a person I would be dealing with for the next ten years.

The Flying Mustache ranch house reflected Joe Miller's Eastern heritage. He had spent a considerable sum to remodel the old adobe house to keep his wife happy in the country and to enable her to entertain in the style that she had been used to in town. The corrugated tin roof was replaced with Spanish tile, and instead of adding bedrooms to the old house he had added another building. Charlie commented that it was the only house he had ever seen where you had to go outside to go to bed. Joe also added a guest house to accommodate his former air force buddies when they passed through southern Arizona. There were five bathrooms at headquarters. I had asked Joe the reason for what seemed to me a surplus of toilets to flush when water was being pumped from a thousand feet down. His reply was, "I built this house to entertain in, so if there are twenty-five guests here, what is the difference between having them flush five toilets five times or one toilet twenty-five times?"

In spite of all the money Joe had sunk into the house to keep his wife happy in the country, after a year on the ranch the Miller family moved back to the upper-class section of Tucson, although Joe continued to play at ranching. In all fairness, I should say that Joe liked the ranching business and the people he met in it. He would have been content to put tags in the ears of his calves and go outside to go to bed for the rest of his life if his wife had not insisted on moving back to town. In a way, I have Mrs. Miller to thank for my first opportunity to get into the cow business.

For man or beast, water can be a distinct problem on the bajada of the Sierrita Mountains. Most of the stock water came from *represos,* earthen reservoirs constructed to catch the runoff from arroyos. Drilled or hand-dug wells are scarce on the bajada because the water table is deep beneath the alluvial fan. There were two drilled wells and one hand-dug one on the O Bar J. One of the drilled wells was at headquarters, and the other was located in the northwest corner of the south pasture. Both wells were a thousand feet deep. The headquarters well was equipped with a submersible pump that filled two large storage tanks at a rate of five gallons per minute. The other drilled well, the Pozo Hondo, was pumped with oil-well equipment, including a Jensen Jack (the type that bobs up and down while operating), which was propelled by a small gasoline engine. This pump produced four gallons per minute when the leather washers on the piston were new. There was also a large steel storage tank at the Pozo Hondo. The third well, the hand-dug one, was sixty feet deep and was located in a corner of the Pacheco pasture. It was not a strong source of water because it depended on an underground dike and a represo above it to retain a certain level of water.

The remaining stock water on the O Bar J was in the represos—some good, some not so good, depending on the rainfall. The Hall Tank was centrally located and held a substantial amount of water. The Rova Tank, in the north pasture near the eastern boundary, was of little consequence as it just held a small amount of stock water for a while after its feeder arroyo flooded, an event that occurred only once during my tenure of the ranch. Miller had constructed two represos in the north pasture, both near headquarters. The represo next to the corrals was ill-conceived, not only because it was close to a permanent well but also because it leaked! The other represo was in the middle of a stand of cholla. It contained about half its capacity when I took over the O Bar J, but for the next two years its bottom was just a mosaic of parched silt. I never saw it full.

One part of my lease agreement with Joe Miller that I had paid little attention to called for me to furnish water to the Black Dike Mine by way of a pipeline Miller had installed from the Pozo Hondo to a storage tank near the mine and the Pacheco Tank. Miller apparently didn't consider it very important since he figured I would be using the pipeline anyway.

In the middle of the pipeline there was a steel storage tank, appropriately named the Middle Tank. It was equipped with a water trough and could be used in the event that the Hall Tank went dry. From the Pozo Hondo a booster pump sent water to the Middle Tank, and then another booster pump pushed the water from the Middle Tank to the Black Dike tank, another steel tank. In theory the pipeline was a good idea, but it was built with only one-inch-diameter pipe, which didn't supply enough water to keep up with the usage.

A minor source of stock water was the Copper Grantz mine shaft. There was a small accumulation of water in the mine, and Miller had placed an electric pump just above the bottom of the shaft. At the mouth of the shaft he had installed a gasoline-powered generator to furnish the electricity for the pump motor. I asked Charlie about the setup, and he informed me that the water had risen in the shaft, covered the pump motor, and made it inoperable. Charlie also said that there wasn't enough water accumulation to be worth pumping. That analysis was good enough for me, for two reasons: I had no desire to climb down the Copper Grantz shaft, and if I had, I wouldn't understand the first thing about operating the pump, much less repairing it.

The Hairballs

he fact that the winter rains never materialized and that there was no spring feed for my cattle did not dry up my enthusiasm for the cow business. I plunged into the daily work on the ranch early each morning and returned to cook my evening meals after the sun had set behind the Baboquivari Mountains. By April it was obvious that I would gain little by holding the weaner calves I had bought with the herd.

When Joe Miller had shown me the cattle, I had been so eager to buy that I really didn't look at the weaner calves too closely because I was more interested in the cows. Mistake number one! I should have looked at the calves to see what the cows could produce, but the green kid had only one thought in mind: to get into the cow business. Miller told me that he was going to do me a favor by selling me the current weaner calf crop and that they would average four hundred pounds. That sounded great to me, the green kid, so I agreed to his deal.

After my decision to sell the weaner calves, Charlie and I moved them into the north pasture to facilitate showing them to prospective buyers. Then I went to town to spread the word that I had calves for sale, and the most logical place to start was the local livestock auction. I spotted Carl Bridger in the coffee shop and approached him. Carl was my neighbor to the south, but he spent most of his time as an order buyer. Order buyers buy livestock for accounts such as feedlots or traders from other parts of the country, and most work on a commission, usually on a per head basis. During the 1950s buying commissions were one to two dollars per head. The sale of my calves involved two order buyers, one from New Mexico, who was buying for a feedlot operator in Kansas, and Carl Bridger, who was buying for the order buyer from New Mexico. Carl and the man from New Mexico arrived two days later to look at what I had to offer.

The New Mexico buyer had been scurrying around southern Arizona with Carl. He was offering two cents a pound above what light-weighing calves were bringing at auction, so I signed a contract for delivery in two weeks. The terms of the contract included an overnight stand without water, a 10 percent cut (a clause the buyer used to turn back the heaviest calves, which were worth less per pound), and delivery to the Southern Pacific corrals in Tucson, where the calves would be weighed "off the trucks." In layman's terms, I was obliged to gather the calves and put them in my corrals without water the night before the buyer from New Mexico was due to arrive at seven o'clock the following morning to cut out 10 percent of the calves from the bunch. After that was accomplished, the calves would be loaded onto the cattle trucks I had ordered, which would deliver the calves to the Southern Pacific corrals, where they would be weighed. The weight times the price per pound would be the amount of the sale. I was to learn much from that first sale of my calves.

Charlie and I gathered the calves the day before the delivery date and put them in the headquarters corrals. I noticed that about fifteen were quite small compared to the others, and their hair was longer. They also looked unusually potbellied. I asked Charlie if he knew why these particular calves were so different from the others.

"They're hairballs," he said. "Their mothers are toothless old nellies that don't give enough milk for a housecat." Charlie then assured me that he could pick out the old nellies from the herd so I could cull them.

"While you're at it," he added, "you might as well dump those cracker-assed bulls that are sirin' sorry calves." From previous conversation I knew the bulls he had in mind.

The buyer from New Mexico showed up an hour late the next morning, giving as his excuse that his alarm clock hadn't gone off. Later I was to realize that this type of behavior was not uncommon among cattle buyers, but that morning I didn't give his tardiness much thought. When the buyer walked into the corral with his rawhide-wrapped whip, and started chousing the calves, I saw what kind of a game he was playing. Instead of cutting out his 10 percent he was chasing the calves around the corral to cause them to shrink more, which meant that he would have to pay for fewer pounds. I would therefore get less money for my calves. I walked up to him and told him to point out the calves he wanted and I would do the cutting. I had reached a point in my patience and newly acquired understanding of cattle buyer tactics that if he had not honored my request I was ready to open the gate to the north pasture and look for another buyer. The man from New Mexico had already broken the contract by arriving an hour late.

After the calves were sorted (the buyer had rejected the heaviest ones), he offered to buy the rejects for two cents a pound less. I agreed because I wanted to get rid of the entire bunch as soon as possible. We loaded the calves into the two cattle trucks and followed them to the Southern Pacific stockyards.

There were several pens holding calves waiting for shipment. We pushed my calves through the alleyways to the scales. I watched closely as the calves were weighed and made sure I wrote the weights on my tally sheet. The calves weighed so much less than I thought they would that I had to go over the numbers a second time. The average weight was 270 pounds, a far cry from the 400 pounds Miller had claimed he was used to shipping. The trip back to the ranch seemed longer than usual as I kept mulling over my first experience at selling calves and the dilemma I found myself in. By the time I drove up to the barn, my stomach felt like an eggbeater was whirring around inside it. I told Charlie what the calves had averaged. He wasn't surprised, and when I mentioned Miller's claim of four-hundred-pound calves, Charlie told me that in the three years he had managed the ranch for Joe Miller the calves had never averaged 400 pounds, even after a good year.

I suddenly knew what I had to do. I sent Charlie out to gather the old nellies and cracker-assed bulls. Then I drove back to Tucson and parked in the driveway of Joe Miller's El Encanto mansion. I wasted no time in telling him that he had misrepresented the calves to me and that I felt he should share at least half the loss I had experienced. Of course, he denied any misrepresentation and claimed that it would be highly extraordinary for him to even consider sharing my loss. Joe Miller thought he was still dealing with the same green kid as he had a couple of months earlier. By the time I left, he realized that I was not as naive as I once was. I drove away with his check in my pocket.

The entire episode gave me far greater confidence, and I switched my thoughts to long-range planning for the O Bar J operation. In the midst of my thoughts, Charlie rode in from the Hall Tank, where he had left the cows and bulls he had gathered. I was not prepared for his latest bad news, though for some reason I never heard any good news from Charlie Moss.

"There's a two-year-old heifer drowned in Pacheco Tank," he said, still mounted on the Paint. "The tank's almost dry and she got herself stuck in the bottom. Damn shame—she was pretty heavy with calf. You should have moved those cattle out of that pasture."

I didn't reply. I felt bad enough about losing the heifer; she was the first to die. Charlie had a way of shifting any of his feelings of guilt onto someone or something else. I wasn't thinking of blaming him until he said it was my oversight. It was my fault because she was my heifer, and I was supposed to be managing the affairs of the ranch. I had not been near the Pacheco Tank for quite a while. I knew at that moment I was depending on Charlie too much. I loaded a long chain into the Jeep and we headed for the Pacheco Tank to drag the dead carcass out of the remaining water. I saw about a dozen buzzards fly up and circle in their waiting pattern as we pulled up to the scene. The heifer looked like she might have been one of the best cows on the ranch. I had a feeling of sadness as I imagined her struggle to keep from drowning.

Charlie broke the silence between us as we neared the gate to the north pasture. "I put thirty cows into the water lot at the Hall Tank, and I gathered the worthless bulls. They're in there with the cows."

"Good," I replied. "We ought to get through cutting them out and back to the headquarter corrals before it gets too hot in the morning."

"It shouldn't take too long," Charlie said. "I've got to go to town this evening to see a friend of mine."

I thought little about his sudden trip to town, thinking he would be ready to work the cattle shortly after sunrise. I didn't know much about Charlie Moss.

After feeding the horses the next morning I began to wonder why Charlie wasn't ready to saddle up for the day's work. I went back to the house and poured another cup of coffee to wait with. Still no Charlie. Then I drove the quarter mile to his house and noticed his car was not parked in its usual place. I didn't stop to ask Henrietta where her husband might be, I just returned to the barn, saddled the Paint, and rode out to the Hall Tank. I gathered the cows and bulls and drove them into the wire corral above the tank. Without Charlie to help with separating the old nellies I knew I had my work cut out for me. It turned out to be easy to choose the cows I needed to sell, and of the eight bulls he had gathered I cut back the one that looked the best. The sun was more than halfway to its early May zenith by the time I had finished separating the cattle and had turned the ones I wanted to keep back into the south pasture. Driving the cracker-assed bulls and the old nellies to headquarters was a slow process because of the midday heat, but I felt good having accomplished the task at hand by myself. Still no Charlie.

I drove into town to order a cattle truck to pick up my cattle in time for the next auction on Saturday. I had decided that the auction would be the most appropriate place to sell that sorry bunch of bovines, and I was hoping that nobody at the auction would take notice of where those cattle came from. On the way back from seeing about the cattle truck I stopped at the Mission Club on Ajo Road, where I had seen Charlie's parked car on my way into town.

Charlie was the sole customer sitting at the bar. He was hugging a bottle of beer. As I approached he turned to discover through bloodshot eyes who had arrived in his presence. Charlie greeted me like a long-lost friend as I sat beside him. He refused my offer to drive him back to the ranch. I refused his offer to buy me a beer and left him sitting on his bar stool. On the way back to the ranch I stopped at the market to buy some food for Charlie's family.

I had just finished feeding the saddle horses the following evening when Charlie drove up to the barn, parked with somewhat of a lurch, and walked up to where I was tossing hay to the old nellies and the cracker-assed bulls.

"You missed a couple cows and one of the sorry bulls," Charlie said as he looked out over the cattle I had penned in the corrals.

"Too bad you weren't there," I said, continuing to scatter the flakes of hay into the long feed trough.

"You can't afford to pay me what I'm worth," he said.

"You are probably right on that score, Charlie. You're a helluva good hand. Are you figuring to quit?"

"I can't afford to stay any longer."

"You've got two weeks' pay coming. I'll bring you a check when I finish feeding."

"How about buyin' those dozen layin' hens? Will you give me two bucks a piece?"

"Sure, Charlie. I'll add that to your check."

I was relieved after that conversation. I had been feeling trapped by the agreement to keep Charlie on the payroll for six months. I had four months left and didn't need to be paying wages to someone who didn't show up for work. During those two months I had made tremendous progress with my ability to make decisions, something I was never faced with as a cowboy working for wages. Someone else had always shouldered those responsibilities. Charlie Moss and family drove away from the O Bar J that evening.

The cattle truck arrived the following morning and hauled my culls to the auction. None of the old nellies had calves by their sides; they didn't even look bred. Even if any of those cows had had calves, that wouldn't have changed my mind to cull them from the herd. I didn't need cows that raised hairballs.

Challenges, Challenges

The market for old cows and bulls held up, and I was happy with the check I received from Gene Payne's Livestock Auction. The Saturday sale day was a good time and place to discover opportunities and to follow the cattle market. I found out about some two-year-old heifers and made an appointment to look at them. They were located at the San Cayetano Ranch near Tumacacori in the Santa Cruz Valley north of Nogales. I was to meet Jason Roland the following Monday to see what he and John Chiapetta, the owner of the ranch, had to offer.

Jason Roland was a trader. He had once operated his own ranch in the Altar Valley south of the O Bar J, but the judge presiding over Jason's divorce gave the ranch to his wife. Ranchless, Jason talked various ranchers into partnerships so that he could buy cattle and have a home for them until he was ready to sell them. Jason Roland was also an order buyer. John Chiapetta, who was his partner on the heifers, had bought the San Cayetano Ranch and had moved there from New York, where he had been in the import business. John knew nothing about the cattle business, so Roland had a perfect partner.

The heifers were in a large corral when we arrived. I walked around slowly, looking at each one. I noticed that half the bunch wore one brand and the other half another. They had originated from two different ranches. Half were horned, with horn weights still attached to train their horns downward. They were from a registered herd, the S Bar S, the San Cayetano's neighbor to the north. The other half originated from the Perkins Ranch near Baboquivari Peak, almost my neighbor. I liked the cattle and could see their potential for adding quality to the O Bar J herd, but I was concerned that they had been maintained on irrigated pasture, and I thought they might have difficulty making a living on the western bajada of the Sierrita Mountains. It would also be at least another month before I could expect any summer rains to bring green feed to the ranch.

In spite of my fears, I decided to take a chance and made an offer for my choice of eighteen of the heifers. Roland and his partner walked to the far end of the corral for a conference. After a bit he walked slowly back to where I was perched on the top rail of the corral, trying to get better acquainted with the heifers in case I had to decide which of them I wanted.

"We need ten dollars a head more," Jason said. "Everyone is going to be looking for cattle once the rains start."

I held my ground on my price, though I knew I would pay the extra ten dollars if need be. Jason walked back to Chiapetta. When he returned he pointed to one heifer that was smaller than the rest. "If you take that small one in your cut, you can have them."

I looked closely at the small heifer and could see that she was not entirely Hereford even though she had the white face and reddish body typical of the breed. Beyond the white face, her eyes and head had the appearance of a Jersey, and she was smaller bodied than other dairy breeds. As a crossbreed she was worth less money than the others. I approached the heifer slowly and noticed that she didn't shy away like the others. "Does Perkins have a Jersey milk cow?" I asked in order to show Roland that I knew what I was looking at.

"Hell, I don't even know if he has a milk cow," Roland replied.

"All right, I'll take that heifer showing Jersey with my eighteen, delivered to the O Bar J."

"Hell's fire, John, I'm givin' 'em to you as it is."

"When can you deliver?" I said with a smile. I knew I had the heifers bought.

"I'll have them up there tonight sometime."

"Okay, let's cut those babies," I replied.

I knew that the Perkins heifers would probably do better having been raised in similar country, and they were most likely already bred. The S Bar S heifers had never been near a bull and looked it. I cut out all the Perkins cattle and took the best of the others.

I drove back to the ranch. That evening, just as I was about ready to give up on Jason and go to bed, he pulled into the barnyard with the load of heifers. We unloaded them and I walked around and among them, looking at my latest purchase with a flashlight. I didn't have any reason to distrust Jason Roland, but I didn't have any reason to trust him either. We went into the kitchen and I wrote him a check. He gave me the brand inspection papers and left. Then I returned to the corral and threw some hay out to the new arrivals.

By sunrise I was busy preparing to brand the heifers with the O Bar J, and I soon had the irons hot. One by one I pushed them slowly into the squeeze chute to be branded. The squeeze chute restrains the cattle for all sorts of necessary operations. The more help one has the better, but I was alone with the job of preparing eighteen heifers to be turned out on the range.

The squeeze chute was located at the end of another chute made of heavy lumber. Once the animals start into the entry chute, it is necessary to separate them with poles slid in front and to the rear of each critter. Getting them to go singly into the squeeze chute when you are working alone is sometimes a waiting game, because you have to be ready to initiate the squeeze action by pulling quickly and strongly down on a lever that locks into place when it reaches a tight squeeze position. Then the animal is restrained and can be worked on, whatever the operation might be. If the operator wants to work on the head of the animal for such operations as dehorning or, as in the case of the S Bar S heifers, removing the horn weights, it is also necessary to restrain the head in a yoke-like squeeze that is directly in front of the body squeeze. Because I was working alone, the branding operation took most of the morning. That evening as the sun was setting and the temperature was beginning to drop, I drove the two-year-olds to the Hall Tank and closed the gate. The next morning I rode south and opened the gate so the newcomers could drift out into the south pasture at their own pleasure.

My next concern was to buy a couple of bulls, since I had sold enough to reduce the ratio of bulls to cows below the point I thought optimum to assure that all the cows would be bred, at least all the cows that were going to breed. Any that didn't breed would go to the auction. I couldn't afford freeloaders on a small operation like the O Bar J. Joe Miller's 65 percent calf crop was not enough to keep my business going. The ratio of bulls to cows depends on the type of terrain on which the cattle are located. The rougher the terrain, the more bulls are needed to insure that the optimum number of cows are bred. Miller had been running one bull for every ten cows. I didn't agree with that ratio because the terrain wasn't rough enough to warrant it. I decided that a 1:18 ratio would be effective as long as I bought good bulls. I bought two breeding bulls (as opposed to bulls not old enough to breed), branded them, and turned them out with the herd. I felt satisfied that my purchases would greatly improve both the quality of the herd and the calf crop percentage, which I sorely had to increase. After that, besides keeping the feed troughs filled with range supplement feed (a mixture of cottonseed meal and salt at a 2:1 ratio, with the one part salt added to regulate the animals' intake of cottonseed meal) and making certain that the storage tanks at the Pozo Hondo and the Middle Tank were full of water, all I needed to do was to check the cattle and wait for the summer rainy season to start.

My next challenge on the O Bar J came as a big surprise. It was also expensive, very worrisome, and exhausting. Miller had told me that the pump in the Pozo Hondo had been re-leathered two months prior to my leasing the ranch, so when no water came out of the pipe one morning late in May I was not only surprised, I was also filled with anxiety.

The foot valve at the bottom of the pump had never been able to hold water in the column pipe, so it took twenty-three minutes from the time the engine was started until the pump began filling the twenty-thousand-gallon storage tank. I always waited to make sure the pump was working, and on that fateful morning I waited forty-five minutes without a sign of water from the pipe. After stopping the one-cylinder engine, I drove down the back road to the Anvil Ranch to ask advice from John King. He recommended that I call G.F. Crane. "Crane is expensive, but he is the best man on pumps. You need the best for that deep well."

G.F. and his two assistants went to work setting up the pump rig as soon as they arrived. The first step in the operation was to lower the sucker rod and attempt to thread the bottom of the pump into the foot valve. To do this, Crane started to turn the rod clockwise with a four-foot-long pipe wrench. Bob, one of the helpers, positioned himself opposite his boss so that the wrench could be passed between them. A great amount of torque resulted from the twisting action, and suddenly the wrench slipped out of Crane's grip and swung swiftly around, smashing Bob's jaw and knocking him unconscious. We were all momentarily paralyzed at the sight of blood streaming from Bob's mouth, but then we carried him quickly to Crane's new white pickup, and G.F. drove hurriedly off to Tucson. We learned later that the blow from the wrench had broken Bob's jaw in two places and knocked out five of his teeth. Had he been standing much closer, the wrench might have killed him.

Bob's emergency left Felix, Crane's other helper, and me alone to deal with the work of pulling 975 feet of three-inch-diameter column pipe, and the same amount of one-inch sucker rod, out of the Pozo Hondo. The stubborn foot valve refused to break loose, so we had to pull the column pipe and sucker rod at the same time. The work was hot and tedious, but we finished late in the afternoon, just in time to see Crane drive up to the well. From the looks of both the column pipe and the cylinder, the three of us doubted that the pump had been worked on for quite a long time. G.F. removed the piston, and the leathers revealed that a new cylinder would be needed. "You just don't put cheap equipment at the bottom of a well as deep as this one," Crane said.

Two days later Crane arrived at headquarters with more bad news. He had made several long-distance calls, searching for an appropriate pump for the well. He had found one in Indiana, but it would take two weeks for delivery to Tucson. The situation called for some quick decision making if I was to avoid moving the cattle in the south and Pacheco pastures to the northern seven sections, which had sufficient water but scant feed. I projected that the storage tank at the Pozo Hondo held a two-week supply of water, but I also had to consider that my projection could be inaccurate, especially if daytime temperatures rose and the cattle consumed greater amounts of water than I had calculated.

Since Crane's rig was still sitting idle, I came up with a plan that could alleviate the dilemma, though it would cost more: repair the pump in the Pacheco Well. The pump jack there, operated by an old water-cooled engine, made the entire setup antiquated, but it might be the answer to maintaining the herd in the south pastures without disturbing them (cattle are always more content when left to their routine). Crane moved his rig to the Pacheco Well, and the following day the old pump was filling the storage tank. Unlike the setup at the Pozo Hondo, which I could just start and then go about other activities, the Pacheco pump engine, being water-cooled, demanded constant attention while operating. The pump jack also needed frequent greasing. Keeping the storage tank filled required tending the old engine and pump jack every morning until midday.

I kept records of the daily drawdown, the water level in the well after a morning's pumping, and the well's recovery after a half day and a night of rest. It soon became obvious that the well's recovery was not keeping up with the volume being pumped, but I could only continue hoping that the new pump for the Pozo Hondo would arrive from Indiana in time to allow me to leave the cattle where they were.

I had been pumping the Pacheco Well for two weeks when, one morning, I arrived to find that the well had recovered a mere ten inches since the day before. The water level in the well measured five feet, and with the pump set two feet from the bottom of the well, I had three feet of water to work with. The hollow feeling again invaded my stomach. I set the throttle on the old engine at the slowest possible speed without killing it and managed to fill the storage tank three-fourths full before the sound of water splashing into the tank changed to the hissing of air. I shut down the engine and left for the Pozo Hondo to check the level in the storage tank there. Sudden ecstasy filled me when I saw Crane's rig poised over the well, lowering the column pipe.

"If nothing goes wrong, we'll have water goin' into your tank before sunset," Crane said as I approached.

"That will be just in time," I replied. "The Pacheco Well just went dry!"

I remained with G.F. and Felix, doing what I could to help get the pump installed and pumping as soon as possible. By late afternoon there was a four-gallon-per-minute stream of precious water splashing into the nearly empty storage tank. That meant that I would be able to leave the herd where they were and not disturb their routine.

The only times the engine at the Pozo Hondo stopped during the entire month of June was when I checked or changed its oil.

Joe Miller was not happy with the prospect of paying his half of Crane's bill for the pump repairs. He was in his usual seat in the stockbroker's office, watching the prices of his wife's blue chips lurch across the screen when I showed him what it had cost to put the Pozo Hondo and Pacheco pumps in good repair. He was unhappy that I had called G.F. to do the work, complaining that he was too expensive. Miller also griped about the cost of the cylinder that had come from Indiana. I let him have his say; my only reply was, "You don't put cheap equipment in the bottom of a hole as deep as that one." He reluctantly pulled his checkbook from his briefcase and wrote a check for half the repair bill.

The fact that Joe Miller had misrepresented both the calves

and the state of the Pozo Hondo pump to me was something I had to keep in the background of my thinking. To challenge his integrity would not have helped me in future negotiations with Colonel Joe, so I returned to the O Bar J to keep the water filling the storage tanks.

To Fight
or Not to Fight

The first summer storm rolled in during the afternoon of the last day of June, but it spilled out a mere twenty-hundredths of an inch, barely enough to settle the dust in the south pasture. The earth continued to burn for several more days until the huge white thunderheads from the south arrived early one afternoon and began to blacken and billow. The rains were spotty, and by the third week in July the clouds were flying high, too lofty for any hope of a storm. Conditions seemed to improve by the middle of August, however. The thunderheads came up from the south at lower altitudes, but they seemed to split over Samaniego Peak, the summit of the Sierrita Mountains. The Pacheco pasture and the eastern end of the south pasture received two storms, and the rain gauge at the Black Dike Mine showed thirty-hundredths from one storm and twenty-six from another. The north pasture was almost rainless.

Again it was time for decisions. I rode over the entire fourteen sections, evaluating the feed condition and thinking of alternatives. I tried not to ponder the possibility of receiving either more summer rains or winter cyclonic storms. I had to focus on exactly what was there, what I could count on, in order to decide what decision would be the wisest.

The condition of the O Bar J's range left much to be desired as far as carrying the cattle through the winter was concerned. Forage in the Pacheco pasture was in the best condition by far because the rains, scant as they had been, had brought growth to the black grama grass and other perennials. The part of the south pasture adjacent to Pacheco was also in fair condition, but the western half was disappointing. The north pasture had not received enough moisture to make any significant contribution to the forage on the fourteen sections. The mesquite, palo verde, and cholla I counted as browse, but there was no grass to go with it. If I chose to fight the drought instead of selling off most of the herd, I would have to buy many tons of range supplement feed. The cattle market had fallen considerably because many ranchers had already decided to sell and wait for the drought to end. If I chose to do likewise, I would get about half as much as I had paid for my cows, and whenever it rained again the price of cows would skyrocket with the increased demand and undersupply. The only cloud in the sky was the dark and dismal one that hovered over me with its huge, unanswerable question: How long would the drought last?

The next Saturday, before the auction, I stopped by the feed mill to see what price I would have to pay for range supplement. The salesman said it would be sixty-three dollars a ton plus a two-dollar-per-ton delivery charge to the O Bar J if I ordered ten tons. I inquired if he could do better if I ordered a larger quantity.

"No," he quickly replied. "I would advise you to order what you think you are going to need for the winter because I can't guarantee that the price of two-to-one will stay put."

"I'll let you know," I said. "I may have to sell off my cows if I can't do better than that."

Cattle prices at the auction that Saturday did little to lift the spirits of anyone in attendance. Calves were selling for nineteen cents a pound for steers and seventeen for heifers. Old cows were bringing around sixty to seventy dollars per head for eight-hundred-pound cows. Nobody wants cattle when there is no feed. I left for the ranch before the auction finished for the day. I still had to fill the gasoline tank at the Pozo Hondo and check to see if any weekend hunters had left gates open. The latter was a routine on both Saturdays and Sundays. I stopped at the Three Points Store before going the last eight miles to the O Bar J. The mail for the week included the *Arizona Cattlegrowers Weekly Newsletter.* My mail was addressed to Box 25, Sells Star Route, which was shared by several ranchers in the vicinity of Three Points. Box 25 was a corrugated cardboard box that had once held a case of Del Monte peaches. Ray Dill, the owner of the Three Points Store, kept the box under his counter.

The newsletter contained short messages, mostly rainfall reports from ranchers around the state. A note from a rancher in the Prescott area mentioned that he was paying fifty-three dollars a ton for 2:1, including delivery, from Western Cotton Products in Phoenix. I was so excited that I postponed the ranch chores and drove directly to the Anvil Ranch to tell John King about the bargain. He was not interested, however, because he had made all his feed purchases from the Tucson feed company for years without questioning their prices. I felt no such loyalty.

I drove to Phoenix the next day to see if the price quoted by the Prescott man was accurate. I found the obscure Western Cotton Products office tucked behind one of the large buildings that housed the machinery used to extract cotton-seed oil. The salesman showed me samples of the product, called Paymaster, in meal and flake form and gave me a short tour of their facility. As I walked around I suddenly made my decision: I was going to fight the drought! I ordered a twenty-ton load of flaked 2:1. The flake form would cut wind loss to almost zero. I took a sample with me to show John King, and when he saw what I had he telephoned the office in Phoenix to order a twenty-ton load of flaked Paymaster for the Anvil cows.

Unloading the hundred-pound sacks of Paymaster from the semitrailer when it arrived left my shoulders sore and aching, but the sight of those twenty tons stacked in the barn made me feel triumphant to have found a reliable and reasonable source of 2:1. I felt even more triumphant the following Saturday when I went to the feed mill in Tucson for some horse feed and saw the same truck that had delivered my twenty-ton load backed up to the loading dock of the mill, its twenty-ton load of Paymaster half unloaded.

Neighbors and
Neighboring

I t takes more than good fences to make good neighbors. The concept of neighboring differs among individuals. From my point of view, neighboring is much more than sharing a common fence. Being a good neighbor means helping and being helped, with neither having the feeling of being beholden to the other.

It is common courtesy among cattlemen to inform their neighbors when they plan to round up and ship their cattle. Neighbors then have the opportunity to look for any stray animals gathered in the roundup that may carry their brand. It is also an occasion for sharing the work of the roundup. The O Bar J had several fence-sharing neighbors and some whose nearest fence was as far as eight miles distant. Along the entire northern and western boundary was John King's Anvil Ranch, the largest and oldest established ranch in the area. The western boundary of the Anvil Ranch was high in the Baboquivari Mountains. The Anvil range included 125 sections. John raised commercial Herefords and maintained a small band of brood mares to produce ranch horses. The Anvil headquarters was located almost directly west of the Pozo Hondo. I spent a good deal of time with John King, talking about the cow business and seeking his advice about combating the drought. We neighbored in many different ways. King was a cowman, and his lifelong experience at the Anvil Ranch and his willingness to share it were great assets for me in my decision making for the O Bar J.

The Anvil Ranch carried a crew of three cowboys, and sometimes four. They were from across the international boundary south of Sasabe. The conversations I had with them improved my ability to speak Spanish considerably because they did not, or would not, speak English. John preferred cowboys from "across the line" because, he said, "They are available and will work."

Along the eastern boundary of the O Bar J were two smaller ranches, the Gunsight Ranch and the Schmeiding Ranch. The Gunsight was north of Schmeiding and was operated by an ex–Arizona Ranger. He didn't own the place, but he would have liked to have everyone believe he did. Ranger worked for his sister. The Gunsight Ranch had no permanent water, which forced Ranger to haul most of the water he needed in a tank mounted in the bed of an old Chevrolet pickup. He would fill the tank at a farm near Three Points and drive up the Sierrita bajada to his place at least once a day and sometimes twice. He did have a couple of water holes for his livestock, but they were not year-round tanks.

Ranger also spent a lot of time sitting in the Three Points Store, telling yarns to whoever would listen. As an Arizona Ranger he had been involved with strikebreaking at Bisbee when the striking miners were shipped off in railroad cars. Ranger was old enough so that there wasn't anyone around to dispute his lies and tall tales. Everyone in the area was well aware that Ranger never went anywhere without his Smith & Wesson.

It was difficult to consider Ranger a neighbor even though he lived on a ranch that bordered the O Bar J. Ranger never informed anyone when he was planning to round up or ship his cattle, so the brand inspectors, aware of Ranger's disregard of tradition and courtesy, would insure that all Gunsight Ranch neighbors knew his shipping dates. I would make sure to inform him when I was planning to round up or ship, but he never made an appearance to help with the gather or check out the cattle I was planning to ship. He probably saw no need to look at what I was shipping because he ran Brahman cattle and mine were all Hereford.

Toward the end of October 1956, I had returned to headquarters, finished the evening chores, and was preparing supper when I heard the dog barking in her tone that told me someone had arrived in the barnyard. I left the stew and beans simmering on the stove and went outside to find a rider still mounted. He raised his hand in greeting. I returned the gesture and said, "¡Hola!"

"Francisco Leyvas, a sus ordenes," he replied.

"Juan Duncklee. Mucho gusto."

I invited him to dismount, put his horse in a corral, and come into the house for dinner. He had told me that he worked with Ranger (Mexican cowboys always used *con,* with, instead of *por,* for, when explaining who was their *patrón,* boss). Leyvas led his horse into a corral as I threw a flake of hay into the manger. *Chico* means little boy in Spanish, and because of his short stature Francisco Leyvas had been called Chico most of his life. We walked back to the house and I poured two cups of coffee. The meal was ready, so I dished out two platefuls and heated some tortillas over the flame from the stove. Chico ate with dignity, but it was obvious that he was hungry. When we had finished our meal he began to tell me why he had ridden to the O Bar J.

Chico had gone to work at the Gunsight Ranch a month before because Ranger was planning a trip to Texas and needed someone to look after the ranch while he was away. Chico had been there for two weeks, and he had ridden in that evening because Ranger had not left enough supplies to last. Chico, at seventy-nine years old, had understood that Ranger knew he would be able to find provisions somewhere in the vicinity, and that would save Ranger money. Chico was not happy with Ranger.

I filled a gunnysack with all kinds of provisions, including a carton of cigarettes. "Whenever you run out of anything, come on back," I said. "Come back anyway, anytime." Little did I know that this old cowboy would be on my payroll in another year or so.

Chico tied the sack on his saddle and rode back to the Gunsight. Ranger must have returned before he used up the contents of the gunnysack I had given him. The next time I saw Ranger at the store I didn't mention Chico's visit.

Several months after I had met Chico, I was riding the north pasture one morning. Near the road to the Gunsight Ranch I saw a cow off by herself and decided to check on her. As I rode up I saw her calf tied down with a piggin' string (a short, thin piece of rope used to tie an animal down). I was surprised at the situation but automatically dismounted and released the calf to go back with its mother. Almost as soon as I'd untied the calf it occurred to me that whoever had tied it up must have had plans to steal it. "Damn it," I admonished myself. "Why the hell didn't I leave that calf tied up so I could catch the cattle thief in the act." I had only thought about the calf's well-being. Then I realized that I could hide behind some trees next to the nearby arroyo, and thief would show up to claim his booty.

I rode to the cover of some mesquite trees and waited. Within fifteen minutes I saw Ranger driving his pickup toward the Gunsight. When he arrived at the spot where I had discovered my calf tied down, he stopped the truck, opened the door, and got out. As he was walking around the front of the truck I spurred my horse toward him. Ranger stopped in his tracks, startled. I reined in just in front of him and felt my anger rising. "Here's the piggin' string you used to tie my calf down, Ranger," I said, and tossed the rope to the ground in front of the ex–Arizona Ranger.

He was momentarily speechless. After pondering his reply he said, "That calf had pinkeye. . . . I was going to get some medicine and doctor it."

"You're a goddam liar, Ranger. I let my calf up, and there was no sign of pinkeye. Get this straight, I never want to see your tracks on my side of the fence again!"

I reined my horse around and headed back for the trees, just in case my cow-thieving neighbor decided to pick up his Smith & Wesson from the seat of his pickup truck. I had spoken my last words to Ranger, but from then on I made sure he could regularly see *my* tracks along the fence.

Bud Schmeiding had originated in Ohio, where his family had done well financially. He bought a small farm in Tucson near the San Xavier Mission and the ranch that neighbored the O Bar J and the Gunsight. The ranch was up from the bajada in the Sierritas, and without a large masonry dam to catch stock water, Schmeiding would have been hauling water from Three Points along with Ranger.

It was obvious to everyone that Schmeiding knew very little about cattle or farming; the two operations were there just to give him something to do besides drink. Bud was a jovial sort and a good neighbor, inviting me to his roundups and shipping days. He never came to the O Bar J for roundups or shipping but always sent José Ochoa. José was in his sixties and still an excellent hand with cattle. The first time Bud came by to tell me he was planning to round up and sell calves, he was accompanied by a heavyset Mexican woman who stayed in the car while Bud and I talked. A week later when I arrived at daybreak to start gathering, Bud came out of the ranch house somewhat disheveled and not too sure of his step. He invited me in for coffee. It became obvious that Bud was on a drunk because after his lady-friend poured our coffee he added a generous slug of rum to his cup.

I finished the coffee as soon as possible and rode to the corrals to join the rest of the roundup crew. Bud stayed behind with his bottle and his mistress. That evening, after corralling all the cattle from the Schmeiding mountain range, I rode past the ranch house on my way home and was glad that nobody came out of the door.

We had finished most of the branding by noon the next day when Bud finally showed up at the corrals. He spoke a few words of very broken Spanish to José and returned to the ranch house. José cut out the calves that were to be shipped the following day, and once again I rode back to pump water and feed cattle. I felt sad for Bud Schmeiding.

My neighbor to the south was Carl Bridger. As I have noted previously, Carl spent most of his time as an order buyer; managing his ranch was secondary. It was six months after I had met Chico Leyvas that Carl arrived at the O Bar J one night at around ten o'clock. I was in bed and nearly asleep when the dog started barking. I dressed and walked out to see who could be in the barnyard at such an hour. It was Carl Bridger.

"I'm starting my roundup at six in the morning tomorrow," he said.

"Need any help?"

"I'd be glad to have you along," he said. "We've got a lot of rough country to gather."

"All right, Carl, I'll see you tomorrow at six."

I returned to the bedroom but not to sleep. I had to get dressed, haul feed to the water holes, and start the pump at the Pozo Hondo. Carl's request was unusual. It was customary to give one's neighbors at least a week's notice before a roundup, especially if help was needed. That gave the neighbor time to adjust his own work to accommodate. Since Carl spent most of his time away from his ranch, I tended to excuse his thoughtlessness, but the next morning I felt differently.

With a scant three hours of sleep, I rolled out of bed to get things ready for the trip to the Bridger Ranch. I had decided the night before to trailer the Paint horse to Bridger's rather than tire him out on the rough country before we even started to work. I gave the horse a generous measure of grain and hay and hooked up the single horse-trailer. The coffee and beans were ready, and I ate heartily, figuring that I would probably not see anything to eat until I returned (that turned out to be a wise decision). The Paint loaded easily and we arrived at Bridger Ranch half an hour early. Who was there to invite me in for coffee but Chico Leyvas. I was the first to show up, and I learned that as soon as Ranger had returned from Texas, Chico had quit. Ranger had had the gall to deduct his provisions from his check! I was happy to see Chico again.

José Ochoa rode in from Schmeiding's shortly before six o'clock, and the three of us sat in the kitchen, drinking coffee and waiting for Carl to arrive from his small house nearby. I became better acquainted with these two men over the next two hours. Just before eight o'clock I suggested that someone go over to Carl's house to see if he was still alive. Both men seemed to appreciate that I could recognize Carl's callous attitude.

Bridger came into the kitchen at eight o'clock with no apology but "That damn alarm clock didn't go off." None of us made any comment as we waited for Carl to finish his coffee.

The only flat surface on the Bridger Ranch was where the buildings were located. The hills were not only steep but also very rocky, and the desert grassland, though showing good perennial grass species, had been invaded by brush. Gathering the cattle was a tedious chore, especially in the heat. One more helper joined us riding a small mule. He was Jorge Moreno, Carl's squatter. It was close to sundown before we had finished. I loaded the Paint horse in the trailer and headed back to the O Bar J. It would be way after dark before José would reach the Schmeiding Ranch.

The Yellow Bird Mine was about a half mile from my south fence line within the boundaries of the Bridger Ranch. I had no occasion to visit the mine until the day Bill Choate drove into my ranch. Bill was one of the local brand inspectors, and he had been told that the old lady who was the caretaker of the Yellow Bird had found an orphaned calf. Bill said the calf might belong to me, so we drove over to the mine in my Jeep. We arrived at the old, dilapidated, board-'n'-bat mine buildings to find the old lady sitting next to a small potbellied stove with the dogie heifer beside her. The woman was feeding the calf Carnation Milk from a baby bottle. The place smelled like a corral, and there was yellow-looking calf manure in various places on the worn-out, tattered rug. The woman said her son would show us to the place where the calf's mother lay dead.

Bill stayed in the Jeep while I followed the son up a steep, rocky hill where a two-year-old heifer was dead and bloated.

I found the brand. It belonged to Carl Bridger, so I cut the hide out where it was branded and brought it back to the brand inspector. Bill told the lady that she could feed the calf but that he would have to inform Carl Bridger of the calf's whereabouts.

I was to learn later that the old lady and her son raised the dogie for four months, buying milk and grain on their own account, until one day Bridger came by and claimed his heifer calf. He neglected to reimburse her for the feed she had bought!

Hunters, Miners,
and Open Gates

Aweek or so after dove season started in the fall of 1957, I rode over to a spot where I saw the awesome sight of circling buzzards and found one of the Perkins heifers dead from a gunshot wound. I called Sol Rhea, the range deputy for the sheriff's office. Sol had the reputation of being able to track a mountain lion over bare rock, but he couldn't find a clue that might lead to whoever had wantonly killed the heifer. However, by examining the hole in the hide of the carcass Sol could tell that it had been made by a twelve-gauge shot-gun. I left the heifer to the buzzards, wondering why a hunter could not distinguish between a dove and a Hereford cow. I discovered that careless hunters are a menace to a cattle raiser.

I could not prohibit hunting in the south pasture because it was state land. The north pasture and the Pacheco were deeded land, but the NO HUNTING signs I posted were usually ignored. A fundamental regulation that hunters are required to abide by is not to shoot within a quarter mile of a building or water hole. The Perkins heifer was killed fifty feet from the Middle Tank, and during the same dove season I had to chase a family away from the Cholla Tank, which was on deeded land. They were sitting in director's chairs on the dam and didn't understand that thirty head of cows and calves were standing a hundred yards away, waiting to quench their thirst.

Weekends were patrol days. In addition to the regular work of feeding and keeping the pumps operating, I drove to every water hole and gate on the boundary fence whether or not some hunting season was current. There was no specific season for jackrabbits. Actually, I welcomed jackrabbit hunters because thirty jacks can eat as much as a cow, and with so little rainfall I needed all the feed that would grow. But jackrabbit hunters don't always observe the quarter-mile exclusion rule.

Jerry Delmar seemed to me to be one of the rare hunters who would drive up to the barn to ask permission to hunt rabbits. He became a frequent rabbit hunter on the O Bar J— until one Saturday afternoon when he drove into the barnyard, opened the trunk, and showed me the hindquarters of a doe mule deer he had killed. "What did you do with the forequarters?" I asked.

"I left it for the coyotes," Jerry replied.

"This is the end of your hunting days on the O Bar J, Jerry. I don't cotton to leaving half a deer for the coyotes."

I didn't see any more of Jerry Delmar, but a friend of his who had often joined him in rabbit hunting came to the ranch about a month later. He had heard about the doe episode and how I had retracted my permission to hunt from Jerry. Oscar then told me how he had seen Jerry armed with two revolvers in twin holsters standing in front of his television set and watching a cowboy movie, trying to out-draw the actors. I gave Oscar permission to continue hunting rabbits, but I said that I hoped I would never see Jerry again.

The dates for deer-hunting season slipped my mind during my second fall at the O Bar J. I was driving a small bunch of cows to headquarters down the arroyo from the corrals at the Hall Tank when I was startled by the swish of a bullet and the blast of a high-powered rifle. I yelled in the direction of the shot, ducked down over the far side of the dun horse, Indian-style like I had seen in movies, and rode around to where I thought the hunter might be. There were two of them with red shirts and hats, and sheepish looks on their faces.

I was still trembling from the narrow escape when I confronted the pair. I explained what they had done and how close they had come to shooting me. I also informed them that they were hunting on posted deeded land and had no right to be doing so. From that day on I was acutely aware of the dates of hunting seasons.

It is illegal to shoot from a vehicle, but the law didn't seem to matter to a Jeep station wagon full of quail hunters in the fall of my first year at the ranch. They were not only shooting within a quarter mile of headquarters, they were also blasting their shotguns from a moving vehicle. To make matters worse, when I chased them down they were impossible to reason with and continued their shooting spree as they drove away. I wrote the licence plate number in my tally book and later turned it over to the county sheriff's office, but to my knowledge nothing was ever done about the matter.

When I found two of the Anvil Ranch horses in the water lot at the Pozo Hondo, I was naturally concerned about how they had entered the south pasture, especially since I had ridden that fence line two days before. I found that the gate on the Copper Grantz Mine road was open. I saw four cars, a pickup truck, and a group of men wearing hard hats standing around talking. I rode up the road to investigate. One man, hatless and wearing a neatly pressed shirt tucked carefully into a pair of khaki pants, seemed to be in charge. He introduced himself as the manager of a mining company that had recently leased the Copper Grantz and said that he planned to ship ore in the near future.

This was my first encounter with a mining operation, but since that time I have learned that when people say they plan to ship ore in the near future, the near future generally becomes later and often never. In the case of the Copper Grantz, it was later because the huge ore truck they had leased carried only one load to the smelter.

The manager promised to see that the gate was kept closed, but several days later I found it wide open again. During the second conversation with the manager, he offered me a job working in the mine. With a depleted bank balance from purchasing such large quantities of Paymaster, I accepted in spite of the trepidation I felt about working in the bottom of a narrow mine shaft. So, for two dollars an hour I became an ore mucker, a shoveler of rocks. I did all the ranch work before and after I went down the shaft five days a week. The manager also paid me five dollars a night to sleep at the mine from midnight until six o'clock in the morning to discourage any would-be thieves.

It was not an easy three months I spent as an ore mucker, night watchman, and cowman. I earned enough money to buy another load of Paymaster for the cattle, but it did not sadden me when the manager handed me and the rest of the crew our last checks with the statement that the Copper Grantz was closed. Neither was I disappointed to watch the last of the miners heading down the road, with the manager the last to leave. He left the gate open.

The first time I saw Lieutenant Crazy he was jogging up the road from the Middle Tank to the Black Dike Mine. I was riding the Paint horse that day and was on top of a hill near the mine, looking for cattle. He was a strange sight, with long blond hair rippling as he jogged along. He wore no shirt, and his trousers were well worn and stained with spots of grease. When he entered the old camp-trailer at the mine, I rode over to find out why he was there.

He was a well-built man and told me his name was Bill. He wore a constant grin on his face, and his articulation was simple and childish. I was suspicious of his presence at the Black Dike until he informed me that he had been hired as the watchman and mentioned the name of one of the mining partners who came to the mine occasionally to putter around. It was obvious to me that something was abnormal about him. I found out a lot about him a week later as we sat in his trailer drinking coffee.

Bill had been a lieutenant in an airborne infantry division that had jumped into Holland during World War II. While there, he had fallen in love with a Dutch girl and had married her. The war went on, and Bill left Holland with his unit and eventually returned to the United States. After seven years he was finally able to return to his wife's home in Holland by hitchhiking to Panama and working his way over to Europe on a Greek freighter. He cried as he told me that his wife had given up on ever seeing him again and had divorced him. Bill never mentioned why he was unable to return to his wife for so long after the war, but his childlike behavior suggested that he may have spent a lot of time in a veteran's hospital from too much war.

The last time I saw Bill he was walking along the road to Tucson. I stopped and gave him a ride into town, where he was going to buy some carrot juice. He said he would be back at the mine in a day or two, but I never saw him again. I thought of him as Lieutenant Crazy not for ridicule but out of sympathy. My conversations with Bill caused me to start thinking about war in more depth than I had before, even after four years as a sailor during the Korean police action.

One day there were different hunters at headquarters. They were not hunting game, they were hunting for yucca, that member of the lily family sometimes referred to as soap-weed. The hunters arrived driving a team of horses hitched to a brightly painted red and green wagon of the old-time buck-board type. They were Tohono O'odham looking for yucca leaves, which they used to fashion their basketry. There was a mother, her son, and two young daughters. The son approached the represo before realizing it was bone dry. I beckoned him to come over to the barn and get his water from a faucet. I also suggested that he drive his team to the barn so that he wouldn't have to haul the two five-gallon cans as far. The lad thanked me with a nod of his head but filled the cans without moving his team and wagon closer to the barn. I went about my business feeding the horses in the corral, and when I next looked out toward the road the team and wagon were no longer in sight. I was happy that I had been able to furnish them with water on their yucca hunt.

I wondered why they were traveling so far for their yucca. Obviously they knew where they were going, so I concluded that the long, gradual bajada of the Sierritas was easier to traverse and harvest than the steeper slopes of the Coyote, Quinlan, or Baboquivari Mountains, which were nearer their home.

Cholla Heaven

Cholla is in the cactus family and for the most part comes in four varieties in the Sonoran Desert. Jumping cholla had found a real home on the O Bar J, especially in the north pasture. The most significant occurrence of this spiny character was a pure stand in the vicinity of the Cholla Tank—a forest of cholla, in many places impenetrable. Jumping cholla derives its name from the notion that the spine-covered segments can seemingly jump and attach themselves to passersby. Nobody ever rides a horse through cholla country without wearing chaps, and even then the rider remains vulnerable above the waist. Wearing a heavy canvas or denim jacket is helpful but not completely effective as protection from the sharp, tenacious spines of this desert species. Cholla reproduces from seed and vegetatively, so it is only "doing its thing" when a segment or segments attach to a human or other animal. It is the cholla's mode of migration.

John Hooperson, who ranched north of the Robles Ranch

at Three Points, and George Halloran, an English instructor at the university, leased the Robles land and bought several hundred steers to raise out there. George had asked me to help with the branding, so I arrived with the Paint horse in my trailer. Hooperson approached as I was unloading my horse and greeted me with, "How are things in Hereford heaven, John?" John Hooperson raised Brahman-Hereford crossbreeds with good success.

"You mean cholla heaven!" I replied.

It was shortly after that that I began burning cholla as feed for the cattle in the north pasture. I didn't just throw matches at the base of the plants in order to burn off the spines; I bought a state-of-the-art weed burner fueled with propane gas. The manager of the propane company came out to the ranch to demonstrate the equipment, and I was convinced that this could be a partial remedy for the poor feed conditions in the north pasture.

A filler hose was attached to the thousand-gallon tank at headquarters. I used this to fill a small tank that fit in the back of the old Jeep pickup truck. The burner was a long-handled device with a pilot light and two burners at the end of the handle. Once the pilot was lit, a trigger at the other end of the handle released large amounts of propane, somewhat like the flamethrowers the military had developed. When the trigger was pulled, the burst of flame was accompanied by a loud sound and heat at 2500 degrees. I could singe the spines from a large cholla plant in a matter of seconds.

The cattle soon learned to connect the boom of the burner with freshly toasted cholla and would come to where I was burning at a trot. There was one bull in the bunch who was always the first to arrive. He was so hungry for his morning meal that there were times when he would start eating before all the flame was out. This habit caused blisters on his nose, so I would periodically put him into the squeeze chute and rub ointment on them. Blister Nose became his name.

I kept one dog, a purebred collie named Nora. In spite of her breed's reputation, she was not a cow dog. In fact, Nora had to be shut up in the house while I was working with cattle in the corral because she would chase the cattle in the wrong direction, barking incessantly. I was convinced that collie breeders had concentrated for so long on the length of the breed's head that a good portion of the dogs' brains had slipped into their noses.

On one occasion I was driving some of the north pasture cattle to the headquarters corral. In spite of a drift fence to aid in corralling them, it was sometimes difficult to get them to go through the gate. I had managed to ease the bunch up to the gate, and one cow seemed ready to enter when Nora came barking and running across the corral straight at the cattle. I could not stop them from scattering away. I rode into the corral, tied my horse to a post, and proceeded to put Nora into the house. Instead of returning to my horse and attempting to gather up the cattle that were already spooked by the dog, I drove the Cholla-burning Jeep into the corral, lit the pilot, and began pulling the trigger on the handle. The blasts from the burners drew the cows into the corral in search of toasted cholla. When they were all inside, I walked over to the gate and closed it.

Burning cholla was a task I performed nearly every morning for two years. By turning this pesky plant into more readily available feed for the cattle in the north pasture, I increased the carrying capacity of the O Bar J during those severe drought conditions. The cattle didn't get fat, but they were able to maintain themselves and raise their calves.

I had read about Texas ranchers burning prickly pear for the same purpose that I was burning cholla. There was prickly pear on the O Bar J, and one particular stand in the north pasture would have provided a good supply for burning, but I had been told that cattle can become addicted to prickly pear. When a bovine becomes a "pear eater" the critter will stand belly deep in green grass and chew on a pad of prickly pear. The spines of prickly pear are longer and harder than those of cholla, and a cow's digestive system doesn't dissolve the pear spines as it will those of cholla. The result is an animal with a perforated intestine and a case of black (from the presence of blood) diarrhea. When that is observed, the animal should be shipped to market before it becomes carrion.

Snuffy Smith was the name Charlie Moss gave to a Thurber bull that had a line-back. This is a color fault in the Hereford breed, and I was surprised that "Mr. Hereford of Arizona" hadn't made a steer out of Snuffy. I suppose that when bull breeders saw Joe Miller in the market for bulls they dumped everything they could on him.

I was looking things over from atop my favorite hill near the Black Dike one afternoon in 1957, during my second spring at the ranch. Across the arroyo I saw Snuffy on a hill, chewing on pear. As I sat there astride my horse, I saw a cow in heat being chased by two bulls. The cow wasn't quite ready, and she was giving the two would-be lovers a good chase directly in front of where Snuffy was eating his prickly pear. He never gave her a glance as she passed him, he just continued chewing. That was enough for me, so I rode over to drive my pear eater to headquarters. Snuffy was so intent on staying close to his meal that I had to take down my rope and swat him on the rear to get him to move.

Early the following Saturday I loaded Snuffy into the Jeep pickup truck and headed for the auction. The bull didn't care much for the ride into town, so he laid down before we reached Three Points. At the first signal light in Tucson I was first in line waiting for the light to change. Snuffy was quite a load for the old truck, so when the light changed I started up slowly for fear of damaging the transmission. A brand-new white Ford coupe was close behind me and gave an impatient blast with his horn. That brought Snuffy to his feet immediately, and he splattered the white hood of the Ford with a liquid black stream of diarrhea right through the rails of the stock rack. I was laughing so hard when I saw the results that I had to pull over to the side of the road once we had crossed the inter-section. I doubt if the driver of the Ford ever pulled up close to another truck that was hauling cattle, and if she did, she didn't show her impatience with her horn.

One time a new instructor from the Range Management De-partment at the university wanted to experiment with cholla and requested that I permit him to conduct his study in the vicinity of the Cholla Tank. I couldn't see how he could do any harm, so I granted him permission. He explained that he was interested in finding out what time of year and what conditions would be optimum for getting rid of cholla by chaining. Chain-ing was a method then being used to eradicate mesquite from desert grassland ranges. The method employed two crawler-type tractors driving over the land with a ship's anchor chain stretched between them. The man from the university was going to simulate the chaining method with an axe! He also furnished a recording temperature and humidity gauge that I was to service once a month. The only thing I had to do was change the graph paper on the drum of the gauge.

At that time I was also keeping rainfall records for a re-searcher from the Agricultural Research Service who was conducting a watershed study. Of the two scientific chores I had agreed to perform, the rainfall recording was by far the easiest because there was so little rain.

One of the instructor's graduate students arrived every

month to chop down all the cholla plants within the measured plots. On several occasions I helped him extract the segments from his back and shoulders. The experiment went through two years and three graduate students.

When the cholla experiment was finished, the range instructor asked me for a copy of the rainfall records that I had been keeping for the man from the Agricultural Research Service. The latter had asked the range man to share the information from the temperature/humidity graphs, and the range man had refused. Therefore, when the range man asked me for the rainfall records, I told him he could get them from the man in Ag Research. I never could understand that attitude among so-called scientists, who are supposedly working to acquire and disseminate knowledge to mankind. In any case, I never read how either study turned out.

Once, after Chico Leyvas came to work with me at the O Bar J, we were after a good-sized calf with pinkeye, a malady afflicting Herefords more than other breeds, mainly because of their facial color patterns. I have seen Angus cattle, however, which are all black, afflicted with this disease. There was no known sure remedy for pinkeye, so most of us attempted to cure it with a wide variety of medicinal procedures. My favorite was sulfa powder, which was sold by veterinary supply houses and some drugstores. Pinkeye can evolve into cancer eye, for which surgery is the only remedy.

I was trying to get a shot at the calf with my rope as it charged away through the cholla-infested desert. At the instant I threw my loop, the calf dodged and the Paint followed, ducking under a large cholla. I couldn't get out of the way quickly enough to escape colliding with it, and I ended up with my right arm stuck to my side by cholla segments. There were more stuck elsewhere, too, causing me no end of pain.

Chico reined in his horse behind the calf and put his loop

around its neck. He had to doctor it alone because I couldn't move my right arm. We rode back to the barn together, and it took Chico an hour to get my arm free with a comb and a pair of pliers. The O Bar J may have been heaven for cholla, but that afternoon it did not fit my concept of heaven in any way.

Win Some, Lose Some

Mucking ore at the Copper Grantz Mine left no daylight hours to ride the ranch and check the herd. I relied on weekends to observe the cattle at the water holes while I hauled feed, kept the pumps operating, and patrolled for trespassers. In addition I was burning cholla on a daily basis.

One day, after the mine had closed and I was able to ride the ranch again, I was checking the cattle in the southeastern part of the north pasture. There was a small bunch of cows and calves that seemed to be holding their own, but I noticed one animal standing alone beneath a large mesquite tree. As I approached I was appalled to find a steer so thin that he looked like a standing skeleton with a dull-haired hide draped over his bones. His head hung low and his tongue partially extended from his mouth, dripping with foamy saliva. As I rode closer I could see the death look in his sunken eyes. It was the worst case of lumpy jaw, or actinomycosis, I had ever seen.

The disease is caused by actinomycetes bacteria entering the animal through the mucous membrane, usually through the gums where tissue has been scratched by spiny forage. The infection that follows causes abscesses along the jaw and often hardening of the tongue (another common name for the malady is wooden tongue). Generally a lack of iodine is present in infected animals. Without treatment the animal dies from starvation because ingestion is inhibited by the swelling.

The only hope for the steer was to get him back to headquarters, where I could lance the abscesses and treat him with potassium iodide. The most serious question was whether he could make it through the mile we would have to travel. I decided to wait for the cooler air of evening to attempt the arduous journey.

Toward sunset I returned to the tree, and Lumpy was still standing in the same position that I had left him, fighting for breath and life. He was reluctant to move at my urging, so I dismounted. By gentle pushing and coaxing, I managed to get him started. We made slow headway because every twenty yards or so he had to rest for ten to fifteen minutes to regain enough strength to continue. A cool evening breeze slipped down from the mountain, and Lumpy seemed to travel easier until we came to a wide arroyo. He sank to his knees in the heavy sand, and in spite of valiant attempts to regain his footing, it was too great a struggle.

I fashioned a sling from my catch rope and placed it around his girth and forelegs. Then I remounted the Paint, took a wrap around the saddle horn, and managed to lift my patient to his feet. I kept tension on the rope during the remainder of our trip to headquarters. It was after midnight when I eased Lumpy into the chute for surgery.

I gathered what I would need not only to operate on the abscesses but also to protect myself. When actinomycetes is contracted by humans it causes bony, calcareous growths in and around the heart. My scalpel was a single-edged razor blade, the surgical gloves were canvas Mule Brand work gloves, and I tied a large bandana around my mouth and nose as an extra precaution. I also spread burlap sacks beneath Lumpy's head to catch what drained from the incisions. I later burned the sacks.

I was working by the headlights of the Jeep. It took about a half hour to lance and drain five large abscesses. The next stage was to pack the cavities with gauze soaked in iodine. I was happy to see that Lumpy was breathing much easier, but he was still dehydrated, so I tried to force him to take some water from a quart-sized bottle onto which I had attached a short section of rubber hose. With a great deal of effort, the steer managed to swallow two quarts. He seemed to know that I was trying to help him.

The following morning it was later than usual when I walked out to the corral. Lumpy was a different steer! His eyes were no longer sunken, his flanks showed that he had been able to drink more water, and he was actually trying to nibble on the alfalfa I had left for him the night before. I knew he was going to make it. The worst was over. I felt a deep respect for that steer's fortitude, and I was exhilarated over my part in saving his life.

I drove into town to purchase bottles of potassium iodide to drench him with to build up his iodine, and I repacked the cavities daily with the iodine-soaked gauze until the wounds began to heal. A month later it would have taken close scrutiny to find any evidence that Lumpy had been so close to death.

Not long after Lumpy's successful recovery, I found a first-calf heifer with her womb thrown out. I had never seen this condition. I couldn't find any sign of a calf in the vicinity, so I drove the cow to the corrals. It took an hour to stuff the sunburned tissue back inside her, pack it with sulfa powder, and suture the lips of her vulva to hold it all in place. I later learned that smearing sugar on a thrown-out uterus shrinks the swollen tissue. Her udder was fairly full, and I was still wondering if her calf might be wandering around looking for its mother, so I turned the heifer loose and followed her. She headed back to the area where I had discovered her, and again I searched for a calf, but to no avail. By nightfall I had decided to pursue the problem in the morning.

The next day, after finishing the feeding, pumping, and cholla-burning chores, I saddled up again to look for the calf. I rode for the remainder of the day and couldn't even find the heifer. Two days later I found her—dead. I never did find the calf. Drought's toll was mounting.

I never saw Crooked Horns with the other cattle at the water holes. She was a loner, and a wild one too. Crooked Horns was a big, thrifty cow and always raised the heaviest calf in the herd, but wild loners are difficult to deal with. To brand her calf it was necessary first to find the pair and then drive a bunch of other cows to join them. Then, if Crooked Horns and her calf didn't bolt and run for freedom, you might get them corralled with the rest. Sometimes it took a couple of tries. Once she was corralled, the only way to get her through a gate into another corral was to stand in the middle of the opening and wait for her to charge. With precise timing I would jump out of her path and slam the gate shut to accomplish the transfer. Sometimes it would take several attempts before I could get the calf in one corral and Crooked Horns in another so that I could proceed with what I had to do with the calf. Crooked Horns was a real pain in the ass. The only reason I put up with her was that she was the best cow on the O Bar J.

The second calf she dropped for me was a nice-looking bull that I managed to change into a steer while he was still only a few weeks old. I would see the pair off by themselves when I made my circles around the ranch. I marveled at how the steer grew and wondered if Crooked Horns would ever calve a heifer. The steer was close to three hundred pounds when I rode up on them above the Hall Tank one morning. I was surprised that Crooked Horns didn't see me, lower her head, and take off with the steer. When I was within fifty yards, she heard me approaching and lifted her head. I saw that her left eye was bloody. Cancer eye! I was really going to have my hands full, not only getting her back to headquarters but also doctoring the eye. If she hadn't had such a beautiful calf on her, I would probably have decided to send her to the auction.

I turned around slowly to keep out of her view, and luckily she didn't turn her head. Then I rode toward the Middle Tank to find some cattle for decoys. There were eight cows and six calves there. I rode through them to make sure I wouldn't be driving any cows to headquarters without their calves, because many times cows will come to water and leave their calves for another cow to baby-sit. I had seen as many as six calves with one cow in such a situation. I started driving the cows toward the spot where I had left Crooked Horns and her calf. If I could get them moving toward the open gate to the north pasture and lure the wild one into joining them, half the battle would be won.

I stayed well behind the bunch once they started in the right direction. One thing in my favor was that Crooked Horns and her calf were grazing very close to the route the other cows were taking, and if they continued the way they were going, the wild cow's good eye would pick them up.

The challenge was to keep my decoys moving toward the gate and at the same time keep Crooked Horns and her calf from spotting me. When the decoys picked up the wild pair, I was watching from a small arroyo. I followed slowly once I was sure that things were proceeding according to plan. Once the cattle were through the gate and heading down the road,

I rode through the gate and began a wide circle in order to reach the corrals ahead of them and get the gates ready. I had to remain out of sight as they entered the corral or Crooked Horns and her calf would run for freedom before I could get the gate closed. To out-think cows, you have to learn to think like them.

I put the Paint in a far corral and hurried to the barn for an armful of hay to throw into the large pen the cattle would enter. After looking up the road and seeing the cattle approaching in single file, I hid myself near the gate but in another corral. Once the cattle were inside, I would have to move quickly.

The lead cow walked through the open gate without hesitation. Crooked Horns was fifth in line with her calf. She had her blind side toward where I lay hidden behind a feed trough. Just before entering the corral she stopped, looked back to make sure her calf was following, and walked to the water trough at the far end of the large corral. I waited until she began drinking and then slowly slid myself under the lowest plank in the corral fence. I had them! I was relieved when I fastened the gate shut. As soon as the gate slammed shut, Crooked Horns jerked her head out of the water trough, wheeled around, and charged. When she saw the closed exit and me behind the gate, she stopped and stood stiff-legged, shaking her head and snorting loudly. The other cows were too busy enjoying the alfalfa to notice their companion's rage. The cancer eye compounded her already unfriendly personality.

It took an hour to cut Crooked Horns and her calf away from the decoys and get them isolated in the pen where I generally kept the horse I wanted to ride, but by late afternoon the decoys were back at the Middle Tank and I was driving to the Anvil Ranch. I knew I was going to need lots of help to get Crooked Horns into the squeeze chute—transferring her from one corral to another was difficult enough. John King said he would be riding nearby with his crew within a week.

When Crooked Horns charged into the working corral like a Spanish fighting bull, neck arched and swiveling around, looking for someone to gore, John and his two men climbed to the top of the fence. "Now I see why you asked us to help!" he said.

Once she was inside the small pen leading to the chute, it was a matter of waiting patiently until she decided that the chute was her only way back to her calf. She pawed the ground and snorted for fifteen minutes before she finally made up her renegade mind to enter the chute leading to the squeeze. She was fast, but with four determined men to operate the squeeze and run poles behind her, she was outmatched. John King offered to do the operation. For that I was extremely grateful. I had never burned out a cancer eye and hoped I never would. If he hadn't volunteered, I would have asked him.

The horn irons in the fire were already red hot. Horn irons are similar to branding irons except that the brand part at the end is replaced by a solid cylinder of iron about two inches long, three-fourths of an inch in diameter, and rounded on the end. Normally they were used to sear the area where a calf had been dehorned. John King pulled one of the hot irons out of the fire and advanced toward his patient, who was standing completely immobilized in the squeeze.

Crooked Horns bellowed as the red-hot metal plunged into her cancerous eye socket. The bloody tissue sizzled as John worked the iron around inside. I had to look away periodically. He picked out another iron and continued burning away all the cancerous tissue. John worked with steady hands that had performed the same operation many times on Anvil cows and bulls. When he was satisfied that no more searing was necessary, John packed the empty socket with cotton soaked with black Smear 62, the old standby screw-worm medicine.

"Do you want to dehorn her while we've got her in the squeeze?" John inquired. "She'll be even more dangerous to work with only one eye."

In spite of feeling that the old renegade had been through enough for one day, I agreed and went to the barn for a saw. I sawed off her horns myself, and we used the irons again to sear the stubs. She jumped out after we opened the front and released the leverage of the squeeze. I kept her in the horse corral for two weeks until the wounds healed.

The newborn heifer calf was trying to get milk from the dried-up bag of the skinniest cow I had seen on the O Bar J. They were near the gate into the south pasture when I saw them on my way to pump water and in the same spot when I returned from the well. If that cow was to live, she needed some good hay. I saddled up and got her and the calf back to headquarters.

I had the smallest of the Perkins cows in the corral to wean the big steer calf she had dropped six months before. Lucy had been named the night she arrived when I was looking over my new heifers after Roland unloaded them. The beam of the flashlight picked up the dust in the air, and Lucy walked up to the dusty beam and tried to lick it with her tongue. "Hey, Luz," I said. "You're a funny one!" Luz, meaning light, became Lucy. Her bull calf became Bozo. I had sold him as a 4H steer prospect for a hundred dollars.

The old cow with the heifer calf became Bones. The thought came to me as I was watching the calf's futility that Lucy might accept the baby so I wouldn't have to bottle feed it. Because I had put Bozo in a small pen away from her to wean him, Lucy's udder was full, and she was bawling for her son to come and relieve her swollen bag. I put the heifer calf and Lucy together and carried the calf over to Lucy's side. The calf wasted no time in getting hold of a teat. Lucy looked around and seemed to welcome the intruder.

Bones didn't seem to miss her daughter in the slightest. She was too interested in the feed trough filled with alfalfa. In the morning Bozo was the only one bawling, but Lucy paid no attention to his pleas. She was licking the little heifer, who was nursing contentedly. Bones didn't notice as the two walked out the gate and up the road.

After two weeks of rest and alfalfa, Bones looked strong enough to make the trip to the auction. When she walked into the sale ring there was a hollow look to her eye. The price per pound that Carl Bridger bid was so low that the check for Bones was only eight dollars. A huge lump crept into my throat as she was prodded onto the scales by the ring man. I suddenly realized that I had done the wrong thing by that old cow. She had tried her best. She had brought the little heifer into the world in spite of her own emaciated condition. She had put so much into that new life that she had nothing left, not even milk. I asked myself why I had not let her die on her range. She had given her calf to another cow, and for purely economic reasons I was trying to salvage what I could from her shell. My feelings of guilt and sadness followed me out into the auction yard pens. Tears welled up in my eyes when I saw gallant old Bones off in the corner of her pen . . . dead.

A newborn calf with its mother was always a beautiful sight. At first the babies are unsteady and wobble on their new legs to find their mother's milk. The mother licks and nudges them to her udder. Within hours the new legs strengthen and the calf finds the source of the warm milk more quickly. The mother cow may stay away from water for several days, but when she decides that her calf is well hidden she will make a hurried trip to her regular watering place, drink, and return to her new calf without tarrying in the shade as usual.

Not all cows are good mothers, however. Some lack the ability to produce enough milk. Others may produce enough quantity, but the quality is poor. Then there are cows that reject and abandon their calves at birth, creating dogies. Dogies are orphaned calves from whatever cause. Drought can be blamed for many happenings, but a cow that will abandon her calf during a drought would probably do it even if she were belly deep in grass.

There was a newborn calf under a tree next to the Pacheco Tank when I drove up one morning. He seemed content in spite of the fact that no mother was in sight. I didn't think anything about it until the next morning when the calf had not moved from under the tree. I walked over and saw that it showed signs of dehydration—it was a dogie. I put the little bull calf into the Jeep and hurried back to the house. There I mixed some powdered milk with water and a touch of Karo syrup, but the calf would not accept it. I knew that he needed intravenous glucose, but I had neither the glucose nor the apparatus to administer it. The closest veterinarian was a man I had known since my youth, so I put the calf on the passenger seat and headed for town, talking to the little fellow all the way, telling him to hang on to his life.

It was infuriating to hear the vet refuse to help my dogie on the grounds that he only treated small animals. The next closest clinic was four miles away. By the time we arrived there, the calf was slipping fast. The liquid trickled into its jugular vein as the doctor listened to its heartbeat through his stethoscope. Suddenly he grabbed a syringe full of adrenalin and thrust it directly into the dogie's heart. Then he listened through the stethoscope again. As he looked up he must have seen my apprehension. "It's dead," he said. "I'm sorry."

I carried the dogie with tears streaming down my cheeks

out to where the dead animals were buried. Later, back at the ranch, I searched diligently for the dogie-making cow, but I couldn't find her. The veterinarian didn't send me a bill.

There are cows that try to become mothers, but as with humans there are a great variety of reasons why they cannot. Sometimes it is a matter of nutrition; at other times the female reproductive network isn't functioning. The best-looking S Bar S heifer was one of the latter, a barren one, but she brought more at auction than I had paid for her.

Another of the heifers breached her calf. The heifer lived, but the calf suffocated before I could pull it out with the fence stretchers, which work with a block and tackle. One S Bar S heifer was heavy with a calf so large that its shoulders couldn't pass through the birth canal when the heifer went into labor.

Since it was her first calf, I had put the heifer in the head-quarters corral to keep her under observation. The morning she started calving, I stayed around to make sure it would be a normal delivery. It was soon evident that the heifer was going to need help because there was only one hoof coming out. I tried to find the other one, but it was somewhere behind the calf's shoulders. I knew that, to straighten the calf around, I would have to push it back in. Even if I could accomplish this, however, there would be no guarantee that I would be able to reach the other leg. After forty-five minutes I had to conclude that pushing a calf in the opposite direction that nature was pushing it was a feat I could not accomplish, but just as the last of my strength was waning, a stranger drove up to the barn.

The man was selling veterinary supplies, and he introduced himself with a reminder that he had been a football star for the university. I told him about the current problem and tried to enlist his help. The football star excused himself, saying he had too many places to visit. He never returned to the

O Bar J. One push from that hulk of a man would probably have been enough to get the calf back inside the womb.

I rushed to Three Points to call the veterinarian who had tried to save the dogie. The only remedy was a cesarean to save the heifer. The doc arrived just in time. The heifer made it, but the huge calf had been en route for too long.

I found it difficult to be objective about my cattle. When they needed doctoring, I did the best I could. If my efforts were successful, I felt overjoyed. If not, I felt sad and often wondered if I had approached the situation properly. After some successes I felt empathy for the animals that had suffered through the ordeal. I knew there would be fewer problems all around if the damned drought would break.

Markets and Marketing

In the jungle of the cattle-buying business, good reputations are difficult to build and easy to destroy with one unethical transaction. By the same token, cattlemen's reputations among buyers are based on the way they represent their cattle and fulfill their contracts. Buying or selling cattle encompasses a broad spectrum of components on either side. It is best to be aware of the market, the various options that are available, and the nature of the people involved in those options if one is going to receive the best possible compensation for the difficult responsibility of husbanding a herd of bovines.

The market for cattle during a drought always favors buyers. It is simply a matter of supply and demand. Demand is influenced by how extensive the drought is. But drought or not, the number of cattle in feedlots throughout the country, as well as local supply and demand factors, can cause fluctuations in the price of calves in the local area. For example, during the dog-track season, old cows held their price because the local demand for ground beef was steady. The old cow meat was too tough for humans but good for greyhounds. When the dogs moved elsewhere, the price dropped. The cow-and-calf operator, the basic producer, receives the smallest slice of the dollar pie, especially when his investment in land, cattle, and effort is considered. That slice can be further trimmed if the cowman selling the calves is not acquainted with the problems of marketing.

There were advantages and disadvantages in selling the first of my own calves on contract to an order buyer. I felt certain that the mood of the fall market would reflect the scant rains of summer, so before the chance of rain that summer waned any further, I decided to investigate the possibilities of contracting my calf crop early. I was also attracted by the 10 percent deposit from the buyer that is customary for such transactions.

I began pondering the idea of contracting early after I arrived home from town one day to find Jason Roland's car parked in the barnyard. I had no idea of the purpose of his trip to the O Bar J but thought it would probably be an attempt to sell or buy. I had no hankering for either with him.

I looked in the barn and corrals without finding my visitor, so I brought in the groceries and started reheating what was left of the morning coffee when I heard the sound of snoring coming from the living room off the kitchen. I followed the snores to find Roland stretched out on a couch, boots standing side by side on the floor, with his hat over his eyes. I didn't try to restrain my laughter. Jason awakened with a lurch and a final snorting snore. "Do you always sleep in strange houses with your hat over your eyes?" I asked.

His face broke into a sleepy grin as he rose slowly to pull on his boots and join me in the kitchen. When the usual preliminary chat was over, he arrived at the purpose of his visit. "Have you sold your calves yet?" He asked.

"I haven't given it much thought," I replied. "I've been too busy taking care of them to think about selling."

"I've got a good order right now, . . . feedlot in California."

Whether Jason really had an order or was just trying to trade on his own account, I didn't know. I waited until he came out with his price. I was interested only because I figured that whatever he was offering, I could get two to three cents a pound more from someone else.

"Like I said, Jason, I haven't decided what to do about my calves yet. I might even haul 'em to the auction," I said. After Roland had made his offer, I had an idea what I might expect from an early contract.

About a week later there was a message for me at the store from Carl Bridger saying that he wanted to see me the next time I went to town. I turned the crank on the rural pay phone, placed the call, and made an appointment for the following day in the Santa Rita coffee shop. At that time the Santa Rita Hotel was a favorite among cattlemen and buyers alike.

I was somewhat surprised that Bridger didn't want to come out to the ranch to look at the calves. I was also quite wary about doing business with a man who kept his neighbors waiting for two hours to begin a roundup. He was half an hour late for our appointment.

Carl was a big man, not exceptionally tall but stockily built, with a moderate paunch built up from too many hours in his car looking for cattle to buy instead of in the saddle taking care of his cow herd. The waitress was prompt with his glass of water and menu. Carl looked more important than he really was. "Bring me a glass of milk is all, please," he said to the waitress. "These damned ulcers of mine are raisin' hell today."

We exchanged a few comments on our concerns for rain and the like before focusing on the business that had brought us together. I told Carl how many calves I would have and what I thought they would weigh by fall.

"I think you might be overestimating the weight," he said.

"Why don't you stop by and take a look at them," I suggested.

"Hell, I know those Miller cattle and have bought 'em before. Those calves have never weighed three eighty. Remember those hairballs."

Bridger offered me four cents more than Roland had, and his offer was two cents higher than the Los Angeles market letter was quoting. I signed the contract and put his deposit check in my pocket. The contract called for weighing the calves at the Southern Pacific yards right off the trucks with no pencil shrink—and no cut! Pencil shrink is a percentage deducted from the total weight to compensate for whatever water and digesting forage the animals might be retaining when weighed. It is one of several points to negotiate in a contract. I was to pay the cost of hauling.

I left Carl with a feeling of accomplishment, but I was annoyed with his reference to my calves as Miller cattle. It's easier to buy cattle in a coffee shop than to saddle up and look them over. I still thought it would have been better if Carl had taken the time and effort to do that. By the delivery date the market had dropped off considerably. I nervously hoped there would be no reneging on Bridger's buyer's part in spite of the 10 percent deposit I had received.

I notified the neighbors that I was planning to round up and ship my calves. I told them the delivery date, but I was going to do most of the gather myself. I didn't need the entire herd gathered, so my plan was to work the south pasture slowly to leave the cattle I didn't need as unmolested as possible. I began a week before my delivery date.

The Pacheco country was first since it was the farthest from headquarters. I had shut that water off the day before. Before working the cattle that were standing around the water trough, I rode the pasture to find any that were still grazing.

There were a few that I wanted, so I drove them to join the rest at the water hole. The rest I left alone to graze. The work was going well. I managed to leave most of the ones I didn't need where they were, and by noon I had the others heading for the Middle Tank to join the cattle waiting for water there.

I was using a basic principle of working cattle that was especially important since I was alone: It is easier to drive cattle toward water than to drive them away from water. As luck would have it, the cattle from Pacheco headed for the Hall Tank. I was able to drop a few of the unwanteds en route. With the Pacheco bunch safely trapped in the Hall corral, I rode back to the Middle Tank and repeated the process. When I had captured all the cattle I could at the Hall Tank, I rode back and opened the water so that those animals left behind could continue with their routine as normally as possible. Once I'd gotten the bunch from the Hall corral started, the rest was easy, and the first day of my roundup was almost over. The sole remaining task was to pump the Pozo Hondo and close its water-lot gate.

I began the second day earlier. Since Crooked Horns hadn't made an appearance the first day out, I knew I had to find the old renegade early and try to use the same decoy system that had been successful before. I found her just before the sun peeked around Samaniego Peak to the east. She and her big steer calf were with six other cows and calves in the northeast corner of the south pasture. I wondered why she wasn't alone, as that had been her usual lifestyle, but I was relieved to think that maybe she had changed personalities after all she had been put through.

Next I rode to the Pozo Hondo. It was early, and most of the cattle had not yet come in for water and feed. I used the time to ride a circle to Pacheco to see if I could discover any cattle I had missed the day before. I managed to pick up three head and drive them toward the Middle Tank before returning to the Pozo Hondo. It was still too early for all the animals that watered there, but I worked them as they arrived, drifting those I wanted toward Hall. When I was satisfied that I had all of them heading in the right direction, I followed. All I could do was hope that Crooked Horns with her six companions would join the bunch I was following.

Before the cattle reached the gate to the north pasture, I circled around them to where I had spotted the old renegade. I had left the gate to the Hall water lot open as an alternative trap. My tactic was simple, but Crooked Horns was not predictable. If I could move the six cows out with the wild one, she might stay with them and join the bunch coming up from the Pozo Hondo. Fortunately, two of the cows were at a distance, and I started them toward the others without arousing suspicion in my principal objective, Crooked Horns. I pushed the two steadily and slowly, hoping the others would stop grazing and start moving out without my having to urge them and maybe lose the ones I wanted most.

Three of the cows had marketable calves with them, but I wasn't about to try to cut back the others. I let them travel at their own pace and direction as I stayed well behind. Crooked Horns and her big steer calf were leading as the bunch approached the Hall Tank. I waited in the arroyo momentarily, hoping she would lead the rest through the gate and into the water lot. Working that old devil cow was like stalking an elk.

I eased my horse out of the arroyo, hoping to see my plan going smoothly, but the old renegade had not even considered the open gate and was leading the others away. My only chance now was for the Pozo Hondo cattle to keep moving toward the gate into the north pasture. Crooked Horns might decide to join them.

From the top of the ridge by the Hall Tank I saw that the Pozo Hondo cows were ambling along, and I needed to get around behind them to keep them moving toward the opened gate. As we came off the ridge I spurred the Paint into a lope to make a quick circle around them. There was no more call to be quiet, so I rode up hard on the rear of the bunch to get them moving. At this point I had to depend on luck—luck that Crooked Horns had decided to act as a normal bovine.

There was no trouble in getting the cows and calves through the gate and moving along to headquarters. Crooked Horns was not in sight, but that didn't mean she wasn't there, because the cattle were lined out and knew they were heading across the wavelike alluvial fan toward water. I didn't have to drive them; I was just takin' up the drag.

I had opened every gate in the headquarters corral complex before starting out that morning and had scattered a couple of bales of hay around in an attempt to tempt the cattle to remain there long enough for me to separate any I didn't want. From my position in the rear I could see that the cattle had spread through the corrals as I had hoped they would. As I approached I saw Crooked Horns in the corral next to the large pen with the long cement water trough. She had lifted her head and was looking around with her one good eye. There were fifty yards and ten cows between the gate and me. I spurred the Paint into a run, scattering the ten cows, but we reached the gate before Crooked Horns could figure out what was happening. She didn't attempt to charge out of the second corral, so I rode in and closed the gate.

With enough experience, one can learn to think like a bovine, but there is always some renegade that has a mind of its own. Now that I had Crooked Horns where I wanted her, I was going to keep her there until the delivery date even if it meant an extra bale of hay. It took an hour of patient work to get the pair into the horse corral with two others for company. That evening I drove back to the Pacheco and south pasture to shut off the water again. I finished up the day at sunset, but before going to the house I looked at Crooked Horns and her big calf through the fence. The calf would weigh at least 470, maybe more. He was beautiful, and I wished I had an entire herd of Crooked Horns even as wild and crazy as she was.

I found four cows with marketable calves the following day and drove them to headquarters. I was surprised that there were only four, but I repeated the same process another day. Then I was finished with Pacheco and the south pasture.

I started early on shipping day. José Ochoa came down from Schmeiding's to help me separate the calves from the cows. We worked them easily, and by six thirty—just before Carl, the brand inspector, and the trucks were due to arrive— I had separated two calves with a touch of pinkeye because I considered them unmerchantable. Since the contract called for no cut, I wanted Carl to see that I wasn't trying to slip anything over on him. I had them penned in the horse corral.

Carl was the last to drive in the barnyard. One cattle truck had already backed up to the loading chute and was ready to receive cattle. Carl and I walked through the corrals to look over my calves. Several were bawling for their mothers, and there were several mothers standing out in the pasture bawling for their babies. As we walked around, I felt a sense of pride. In spite of the drought, I had managed to raise a nice calf crop.

"Goddam, John," Carl said as we ended our tour through the corrals. "I wished I'd a come out here and looked at these calves before I gave you such a high goddam price. They're a helluva lot heavier than I figured they'd be. What have you been doin' to these Miller cows to get these calves out of them?"

"They're my cows now, Carl," I said.

Bridger looked at the heavier calves to see if he could find anything about them that he could call unmerchantable. I showed him the two with pinkeye I had separated. The steer was on the light side, so Carl told me to go ahead and include him with the shipment. The heifer was heavy, and her eye was better than the steer's, but Carl didn't want her. I didn't mind his refusal of the heifer; she had the makings of a good cow.

We loaded the calves, and the two cattle trucks drove away. I knew I had plenty of time to get to the Southern Pacific yards before the trucks, so I leisurely unsaddled the Paint horse and fed him.

When I arrived at Three Points, the two cattle trucks were parked and idling, with no drivers in sight. I entered the store to find the two eating Twinkies and drinking soda pop. "What in hell are you two doing suckin' up soda and fillin' your guts while my cattle are out there on your goddam trucks shrinkin'! Who in the hell do you think is payin' you?"

I turned and walked out the door, surprised at myself, and at the same time glad that I hadn't remained calm. The drivers followed quickly with their breakfasts in their hands. They were rodeo hands waiting to try their luck in upcoming rodeos in the Southwest. In the meantime they were driving cattle trucks, but they obviously had no inkling of how to perform their jobs correctly. I wondered if they had been told to take their time. I followed the two cattle trucks into Tucson and east on Twenty-second Street to Cherry Avenue, where we turned south for about a quarter of a mile to the Southern Pacific stockyards. I watched the drivers unload their trucks.

In spite of the delay at Three Points, Carl didn't arrive until a half hour after the two rodeo hands had unloaded the trucks. I was still so annoyed that I just sat in my pickup truck while the calves went into the large complex of lanes and corrals. I knew I couldn't do anything until Carl arrived, and it further angered me not to see him. The more time it took to weigh the cattle, the more they would shrink and the smaller my check would be.

Carl claimed a flat tire as his excuse for tardiness. By that time I wouldn't have believed any excuse. I was as surprised as Carl when we walked together into the stockyards and found that the calves had been put into a corral with a trough full of water! Walt Steen, the stockyard boss, was standing in the alley. "Get those bastards out of that wet corral!" Carl yelled.

I helped push the calves out of the corral and into the alley leading to the scales. The rounded bellies full of water gave me a feeling of elation. Bridger had done everything he could to shrink my calves, but getting to the stockyard late with his feeble flat-tire excuse was humorous. If he had played straight with me, the calves would not have filled themselves with water.

After the calves had been weighed, we both began doing our figuring. They averaged 387 pounds, just about what I had estimated to myself back at the O Bar J. I refused Carl's plea for a pencil shrink. The fact that the calves had been turned into the wrong corral was no fault of mine. I had lived up to the contract in its entirety. I wondered if Carl bought some new tires with the buying commission he made on my calves.

I went downtown to the bank. Before depositing the draft, I asked the livestock loan officer to check it to make sure it would clear. After a short time he returned to his desk. "It will clear all right," he assured me. "Why would you think Carl would try and fly one past you?"

"Just checkin'," I said. "Thanks."

While driving back to the ranch from town I pondered about a lot of things, especially marketing. While attending the university I had enrolled in a course called Livestock Marketing taught by the chairman of the department. I remembered how his lectures were straight from the text. Neither professor nor textbook mentioned such things as pencil shrink, finagling order buyers, or Twinkie-eating rodeo-hand truck drivers—probably because the professor had never marketed any cattle.

Since the day I had written Joe Miller the check for the O Bar J cattle, I had learned more about the cow business than I could ever learn from being a cowboy, working for wages, or taking all the animal husbandry courses offered by the university. The stark reality of drought required the best of my problem-solving ability; the problems of marketing—compounded as they were by the drought—were a major demand on my thoughts, second only to husbanding the O Bar J cattle.

Hail to the Chief

Cattlemen are not easily organized, or for that matter manipulated. They are as different as individuals anywhere, but there is a certain perceptible ruggedness to that individualism. There are, however, cattlemen's organizations on the county, state, and federal levels. Like many organizations, they are not paragons of democracy, because the elected officers are always chosen by a nominating committee, not the membership at large, and a grooming process seems to be involved with the annual selection of officers. I joined all of them, but after attending a couple of meetings I merely sent in my annual dues. The social life and politics of these organizations did not attract me, and I concluded that my time during the drought would be better spent managing the ranch.

When I read in the state association's newsletter that efforts were being made to have Ike visit the state to see for himself the effects of the drought and possibly to obtain some sort of drought relief for cattlemen, I wrote to the president. I invited him to visit the O Bar J if he wanted to see what was happening—or actually, what was not happening as far as rainfall was concerned. I thought that would be the end of it, and it was, except for a letter from Sherman Adams, Ike's chief of staff. The letter thanked me for the kind invitation but said that the president would not have time to visit my ranch.

The Tucson newspapers ran the announcement of Ike's planned arrival to see for himself the results of the drought. The presidential aircraft was to land at Davis-Monthan Air Force Base. On that particular morning it sprinkled rain on the air base as the president's aircraft pulled up on the tarmac. There was not the slightest threat of rain on the O Bar J.

The following morning I hastened to Three Points to read what had transpired, if anything. The article gave the names of two prominent cattlemen who had conferred with Ike. I noted that one of them was no longer in the cattle business but worked in a bank. The other always seemed to have more money than his ranch would ever produce. The president canceled scheduled visits to nearby ranches because of the rain. Ike's visit to evaluate the drought lasted a little over an hour. Nevertheless, in spite of the labyrinth of government bureaucracy, Arizona was declared a "drought disaster area" and a drought relief program for cattlemen was promised.

The particulars of the program were announced by most of the politicians in the state as if they were personally responsible for obtaining the relief. I read them over and concluded that the entire scam was a program to get rid of surplus grain in government storage facilities rather than to provide meaningful drought relief for cattlemen. The plan was a colossal government boondoggle authored by people in Washington who had no knowledge of what we needed to fight the drought on the parched Arizona ranges.

Cattlemen could buy hay and receive $7.50 a ton back from the government, and they could buy various surplus grains and receive $1.50 per hundredweight back from the government. The program did not specify price controls for these commodities, so the price of hay immediately rose ten dollars a ton, and the grains involved rose two dollars a hundredweight. The result was that hay and grain would cost more to the rancher with the relief than they had before the program was initiated! I felt happy that my barn was full of hay and that I had already purchased a ton of rolled barley for my saddle horses.

What we really needed was cottonseed meal. John King thought the entire thing would create too much paperwork to be worthwhile. I had thought a lot about the program. "I hope a bunch of ranchers go for the drought relief," I said. "If they buy the surplus crap, it will lower the demand for Paymaster, and the price of meal will stay put."

"I hadn't thought about it from that angle," John said. "Good point. Hope you're right."

The drought relief program didn't work, for two major reasons. First, we needed help buying cottonseed meal, but the drought relief included only surplus grains that were of little use as range supplement. Second, there should have been some sort of price control on the hay and grain included in the program. Instead, we continued to buy loads of Paymaster at the same price as we had been accustomed to paying. I also continued burning the spines off cholla. The winter rainy season stubbornly failed to materialize.

Shortly after I shipped the calves Carl Bridger had bought, the Los Angeles Stockyards closed permanently, and along with it went the market report that was the basis of the lease I had with Joe Miller. I went to see him. Besides the absence of the report, I discussed the drought with Colonel Joe. And I was surprised to hear what he had to offer. He lowered the rent payments more than 50 percent. That was better drought relief than the government could come up with.

I had also discussed cleaning out the Hall Tank with Miller. When that major represo dried up, I could see how much it had silted in. The only time to work on one of these reservoirs is when it is empty and dry. But the major problem when tanks are dry is getting the money to do the work of cleaning, because a dry tank generally means drought, and during drought there is the major financial drain of buying feed to supplement the paucity of the subnormal range resources. All this leaves little money for major maintenance projects. Through the Department of Agriculture's Soil Conservation Service, however, cattlemen had the opportunity to receive subsidies for such improvements, just as farmers could obtain aid to level land or construct cement-lined irrigation ditches. I had investigated the idea of cleaning the Hall Tank. I gave Miller the figures, and he agreed to share any cost not covered by the government's contribution.

I started the paperwork in motion and talked to Roy Rucker, a contractor who specialized in earthmoving. The Soil Conservation man came to the Hall Tank to survey the elevations needed for the project, it was soon approved, and Rucker arrived with one of his large bulldozers and started work. We had decided that the material from the process of deepening the tank would be best used as a second wall in front of the hole to further trap the inevitable sand carried by the arroyo during a flood.

Rucker charged by the hour for the work, but I had neither the time nor the inclination to stand around and watch the operation. I did stop by to see what progress he had made toward the end of the first day. The tractor operator had moved the silt layer over to one side so that it could be put back in the bottom, helping to seal the tank against leakage. Then he had started on the cleanout. In spite of the cracked, dry silt that had covered the surface of the empty tank, the ground below was still very moist, and I noticed that the tractor did more slipping than pushing. I watched until the operator shut down for the day. "It looks to me like you're slipping more than you're pushing," I commented.

"Yea, the grousers on this rig are plumb wore out," the operator replied. Grousers are the treads that provide traction on crawler-type tractors, and if they are worn out, there is little traction. I had operated a crawler tractor once, so I knew enough to realize that since Rucker had sent out a tractor needing new grousers to clean out slippery ground at a steep angle, I was not getting my money's worth. Not only that, I would run out of money before the job was half completed.

"Tell Roy that I think he needs to send another machine to do this job," I said.

"I'll tell him what's going on, but all the other tractors are out on jobs right now," he replied.

I didn't think Rucker was trying to cheat me; he was just overextended and lacked organization. However, when I drove by the following morning and saw the same tractor being operated by the same man, I began to question my previous conclusion. I stopped the Jeep and hailed the man to stop. "I thought you and I agreed that you needed a tractor with decent grousers to get this job done without spinning your tracks all the time?" I shouted over the noise of the idling diesel.

"I told Roy when I got back yesterday, but he said he didn't have another tractor to put out here, and to go out and do the best I could," the man replied.

"Well, you might as well go back to town and tell Roy I'm not paying for slipping time."

"You probably won't get this job done," he said.

"This job will never get done with this worn-out tractor," I said. Then I left the Hall Tank to pump water at the Pozo Hondo.

Rucker showed up at headquarters the next morning. "What are we going to do about that worn out tractor of yours?" I asked.

"I went down there to look at it, and I'll have to admit that we need one with decent grousers. The problem is that all my tractors are out on jobs," he said. "Why don't you let me keep on with this one, and I'll charge you half the rate?"

"Look, Roy," I replied. "Let's face it, that tractor in that slippery tank is not worth a third of your rate. Why don't you wait on this job until you have a tractor with grousers to do it right?"

"Suppose it rains in the meantime?"

"Roy, it's not going to rain. Hell's fire, how long will it take to free up another tractor?" I said.

"A couple weeks or so."

"It isn't about to rain in a couple weeks, and if it does I would bet there wouldn't be enough to run the arroyos!"

They loaded the grouserless tractor and hauled it back to town. The two weeks would allow further drying to make the work easier and faster. There wasn't a sign of rain during those two weeks of waiting or the days they worked, and the cleaning operation was successful. The Hall Tank stood fifteen feet deeper than when the bulldozing began, and there was a second sand trap to help settle the sand out of the arroyo's cargo if that cargo ever arrived. What was needed more than anything was rain—a break in the drought! There was a small storm a month later, but the Hall Tank stood ready but empty for the better part of a year. It was beginning to look like we needed Ike to fly in to make it rain.

Too Tough for Some

Ranger was the first neighbor to call it quits. Ray Dill told me that he'd sold everything to Jason Roland and was moving to Texas. That was the best news I ever heard from Ray. With Ranger in Texas I wouldn't have to worry about having a cow-thieving neighbor anymore.

Skeet Root, one of the brand inspectors, stopped by one day to tell me that Ranger was shipping. I waited for an hour before driving to the Gunsight to see what Ranger had gathered. There were four riders, including Roland and Ranger, one of whom I recognized as José Ochoa. The fourth rider looked like a rodeo hand. Skeet was sitting on the corral fence, checking the brands on Ranger's Brahmans. I didn't blame him for staying out of the corral because there were some feisty-looking cattle in there. I walked over to see if there were any white-faced animals mixed in "by mistake."

"Is this all of them, Skeet?" I asked.

"They said there's seven head still out," he replied. "Too wild to catch."

I heard the sound of the first cattle truck in the distance. My Jeep was in the way, so I got in and drove away. I met a bobtail cattle truck down the road and pulled out of the way. The Gunsight loading chute could not accommodate a semi-trailer, so all of Ranger's cattle would have to be hauled in several trips by this smaller vehicle. I wondered if Roland had bought the cattle by the pound or by the head, because the delays would increase the shrink. The next Saturday's auction was interesting. Most of the cattle that sold wore the Gunsight brand.

Jason drove into my barnyard a week later. I had just come in from riding the south pasture. "Did you ever catch those seven wild ones of Ranger's?" I asked.

"Those bastards are wilder than deer," Roland said. "We got four of them. Roped and dragged 'em out. There's three still out there."

"I suspect you can always shoot 'em and butcher 'em out where they fall," I said laughingly.

"Those sonsabitches have run so far and wide they'd be too tough to chew!"

"Why not get Chico Leyvas to help?" I suggested.

"I already asked him, and he said he wouldn't ride for Ranger for a hundred dollars a day," Jason replied.

"I can't say that I blame him. I wouldn't either."

Bud Schmeiding drove up in his pickup a week later to ask me for help rounding up. He was selling everything too. His girlfriend was sitting next to him. I told Bud I would give him a hand. He looked defeated, but I felt that it was not a sincere appearance. I felt more sadness about José Ochoa losing his job than I did for Schmeiding.

In spite of their having only one water hole to deal with, the roundup took three days. Bud rode only on the first day. On the morning of the second day, José and I rode out alone to gather the cattle we had missed. The trucks were waiting to be loaded by nine o'clock the following morning. Schmeiding sold all his cattle through the auction and I never saw him again.

Bridger didn't sell, he bought! I found it hard to believe that he had brought in forty young Texas cows and turned them out on his pile of rocks. Six months later they had all died, all forty head.

My two neighbors selling out didn't give me any thoughts about selling. I knew I would need to cut down numbers, however. The only question was what to sell. I had already sold off all the old cows, and there was a good average age to the herd. I didn't like the thought of selling my replacement heifers; they were all from good cows. Finally, it made better sense to sell the heifers because they wouldn't have calves of their own for at least a year and a half. The mature cows would furnish a calf crop and thus a cash flow. I had put all the heifers in the Pacheco pasture to keep them away from the bulls. By selling them I could open that better country for the rest.

I met a farmer from Casa Grande who was buying calves through the auction. He came out to look at the heifers and bought them. Since he could not be at the Rancho Robles scales to take delivery, I agreed to have the brand inspector certify the weights, and I would deliver the heifers to his farm. There were not enough heifers to fill a semi, so I decided to hire Vernon Mounce with his bobtail truck. I also planned to ship from the Pacheco corral, but that meant I would need to build a loading chute there.

The morning before my delivery date, I had all the heifers penned inside the wire corral at Pacheco. I rode back to haul a few bales of hay to keep them as contented as possible. I didn't trust the wire corral, and if they were to break through the fence I would have a truck but no cattle to load. All this took more time than I had anticipated, so it was almost dark by the time I returned with the tools and materials to construct the temporary loading chute.

At least I had the light of a full moon to work with through the night. I discovered that building a loading chute, temporary as it was, took far more time than I had planned. It was just an hour before Vernon was due before I was satisfied with my work. I built a fire and made a pot of fresh coffee, exhausted from working through the night by moonlight.

I heard the truck groan up the hill to the Black Dike Mine, and it came in sight as it bumped down the hill to the Pacheco corral. There was little maneuvering space to get the truck backed up to the chute, but Vernon managed without burying the wheels in the soft, sandy arroyo. Then I took some heavy wire and attached the chute to the rear of the truck. I walked slowly into the pen with the heifers to start them into the truck, but they balked at the incline and the plank ramp. Vernon went to the cab and came out with a Hot Shot, a battery-powered prod that shocks an animal when it touches him. Just about every stock-truck driver had one to convince balky cattle to travel up loading chutes. I told Vernon to hold off using the device because my greatest fear still was spooking the heifers through the flimsy wire corral.

I singled out the lightest heifer and quickly roped her. We led her halfway up the chute. "See if you can hold her here, Vernon," I said, "and when the others see her ass, they might follow."

Carefully I walked around the rest of the heifers to head them for the chute entrance, whistling to let them know I was behind them. Finally, after about five minutes, a heifer sniffed warily at the end of the chute, saw the one halfway up, and ventured up the ramp. Vernon pulled his heifer into the truck, leaving the rope around her neck. To my great relief, the rest followed. I retrieved my rope while Vernon fastened the tailgate securely. After unwiring the chute from the rear of the truck, I yelled up to Vernon that he was clear. As the truck pulled away, I watched my chute slowly lean over and fall into the bed of the arroyo.

I followed Vernon's bobtail in the Chevy to Rancho Robles and had them weighed. They averaged close to 450 pounds. Then we headed out to the farm in Casa Grande. The farmer seemed to like the cattle I had delivered. I put his bank draft in my pocket and went home. I had worked steadily for thirty-six hours. I didn't go to the Pozo Hondo to check it out when I arrived. I just went to bed and slept for twelve hours.

I left the collapsed chute for a week before dismantling it. When all the boards were loaded, I walked a ways up the road into the Pacheco pasture. This was my hole card. Without it in my hand, I would be playing a bluff. But hole card or not, if the drought didn't break I would have to follow my neighbors who had sold their herds.

Francisco Leyvas

One Sunday I returned from a hunter patrol to find a car I didn't recognize parked in the yard. Neither did I recognize any of the passengers until Chico Leyvas greeted me. I hadn't seen him since Bridger's roundup, but I assumed he was still working there, so I was somewhat surprised when Chico asked if I had any work for him.

I had given no thought to hiring anyone since an experience I had with a man who had claimed to have worked on many ranches. I soon discovered that he didn't even know how to set a fence post in the ground. I was at a loss for a reply to Chico's question. The fact crossed my mind that all the feeding and pumping robbed me of time to check the cattle, so I invited my former neighbor to join me in the kitchen. That would give me time to think about hiring him.

He told me why he had left Bridger. About a month after the roundup, Chico had taken sick and had gone to town for two weeks but had sent his son out to the ranch to take care of things. In spite of that, Carl had deducted two weeks' wages from Chico's check. He had quit immediately.

Heating the coffee gave me time to think. I thought about trying my hand at order buying to bring in extra money. I thought about finding a management job that would not take up all my time. If I explored these avenues, I would need someone to take good care of the herd, and Chico Leyvas would be the best I could hope to find.

I asked him how much I needed to pay him. Without hesitation he said, "Ochenta," eighty.

"When do you want to start work?"

He told me he had brought his saddle and his gear. He was ready to start in the morning. Chico opened the trunk of the car, lifted out a battered old saddle, and carried it into the barn. I told him where the cowboy house was and to help himself. I could tell that Francisco Leyvas was happy to be working at the O Bar J. For me it was the start of a unique relationship I shall always treasure.

Chico had turned eighty the month before he came to the O Bar J. I was twenty-seven. He spoke no English. I spoke enough Spanish to get by. Chico carried a particular kind of wisdom. He not only shared that wisdom with me, he also taught me the Spanish to understand it.

I joined Chico for coffee almost every morning. Those were fascinating times, listening to his stories of the wild cattle he had roped, hobbled, and snaked out of the mountain country bordering the San Pedro Valley north and east of Tucson. He also told me about growing up along the Río Yaqui in Mexico and coming north to Arizona at the time of the Mexican Revolution. He had been young then and looking for work on the ranches. One ranch was still run by Ope Parker, who Chico said was so cheap that he wouldn't keep a wrangle horse because it would cost him a flake of hay. Ope would say to Chico in the evening, "Vámos arreglar los caballos a las tres en la mañana" (Let's gather the horses at three o'clock in the morning). "I had to walk out in the pasture and track the horses in the dark by the fresh horse shit on the rocks," Chico said. He finished that story by telling me that there were two men he would never consider working with again: Ope Parker and Carlos Bridger. I could find no fault with that thinking.

I never had to tell Chico what to do. He would always inform me what he planned for the day's work. I soon found out that pumping water or feeding 2:1 were not part of his responsibility on the O Bar J. He considered himself a cowboy, and in his mind, his job was to ride—nothing more, nothing less. I knew he was caring for my cattle as if they were his own, and I couldn't ask for more than that. Chico kept me constantly informed about the cattle, and I kept the pumps operating all the time, hauled the sacks of Paymaster to keep the feed troughs full, and toasted cholla.

Chico approached me one afternoon after I returned from the south pasture. He had put the heifer that had once belonged to Bones in the horse corral. She had grown well from the rich milk given by Lucy, her adopted mother. Chico asked if he could buy the heifer for his *nietos,* grandchildren. Chico had married while he was cowboying with the Three C Ranch near Oracle, north of Tucson in the Catalina Mountains. A daughter arrived first, then a son. Chico's wife died when the children were quite young, so he had raised the two by himself. The daughter was the mother of his grandchildren. He explained that his son-in-law had been laid off by the mine, and times were tough. He wanted to make sure that his grandchildren never went hungry. He said he could pay eighty dollars for the heifer, and his family could come out the next Sunday to butcher her. The eighty dollars would be his next paycheck.

I agreed to the sale. His family arrived, butchered the heifer, and returned to Tucson with the carcass. When I came back to the barn, Chico was saddling up to ride. "Did they leave you any meat?" I asked.

"They gave me the liver," he replied. "I let them take the heart."

Next payday I handed Chico his check for eighty dollars. "¿Y la vaquilla?" (And the heifer?)

"Call it a bonus," I said.

Francisco Leyvas was a gentleman. I found him to be one of those few, rare among men, men. He was totally honest, totally ethical, and sensitive to others in every way. I still feel honored to have been able to work with Chico and to know him as a friend. I have known some learned men, but Francisco Leyvas had a particular wisdom that can only be gleaned from particular experience with particular attitudes. Every month he signed his pay-check with his *x*.

Watching Chico use his forty-foot-long braided rawhide *reata* was a unique experience. One day we were after a cow with pinkeye. Chico had spotted her the day before, so he knew that she watered at the Middle Tank. We rode through the cattle around the Middle Tank corral at about ten the next morning. The pinkeyed cow was standing in the road. Chico took the coil of rawhide in his left hand and deftly shook out a large loop before approaching the cow. I took my nylon rope from the saddle horn and waited. When Chico was maybe twenty feet from the cow, he swung his loop twice and threw as the cow started to trot away. The rawhide sung through the air and found its mark around the cow's head. As Chico dallied (which involves wrapping the rope around the saddle horn three times), I had my loop ready to pick up the heels. I missed the first try, but on the second I had both hind legs in my loop. We then stretched out the cow until she went to the ground. After that it was just a matter of putting sulfa powder in her bad eye to attempt a cure. With that accomplished, we let her up to go about her daily routine. At eighty years old Chico was still a master with a rawhide reata and an expert at working cattle with the least excitement to them.

Respite

June burned. The air was hot and searing. The ground was hot and powder dry. Even the cholla looked lifeless. We started our days at four in the morning in order to quit early and head for shade.

Tradition says it rains on June 24, San Juan's Day. San Juan's Day came and went without a single cloud in the sky. "To hell with tradition," I was thinking. I burned cholla just like any other day. There were some who maintained that since the Mexicans celebrated San Juan's Day, rain always came to spoil their picnics. Since the Gadsden Purchase the Fourth of July has been the day to welcome the first of the summer rains to spoil picnics. "To hell with the Fourth of July, too." It came and went without even a wisp of a cloud.

The days over 100 degrees seemed never-ending. Nights cooled but little. Then one morning toward noon, about a week after the disappointing Fourth, I saw the first promising thunderheads appear. By late afternoon I was watching the sky fill with huge, magnificent white clouds—moist air masses carried from southern seas northward to the land. These first were riding too high for the convection from the burning land to stop their northward flight, raise them quickly, and cool them to dew point and condensation. But there would be more the next day, and the next.

For four days I watched the sky fill with clouds from daylight until the setting sun painted the horizon with reds, oranges, purples, and blues in a color spectacular. The third day the promise of rain was fulfilled for some, but the O Bar J continued to swelter under the intense heat of mid-July.

The morning of the fourth day, Chico and I had little to say to each other. Neither of us had shaved for a week, and a growth of white whiskers covered his dark cheeks, jutting chin, and slightly curled upper lip. His old eyes, which had watched clouds for so many years, looked tired yet understanding. There was no need for words; Chico Leyvas knew my thoughts, my constant hunger for rain to drench the O Bar J range and wash the dust from the hair of two hundred cows.

The sky was cloudless as the first morning light opened the blackness of night. We walked to the corral with our thoughts. I loaded the sacks of Paymaster into the trailer and filled the gasoline can to pump the Pozo Hondo. Chico was throwing his saddle onto the back of the Paint as I drove out for the south pasture.

There were no cattle in the water lot; it was too early. They were still browsing before the midmorning heat and thirst would bring them drifting in over familiar trails, dust puffing up from their hoof steps to cover their hocks and flanks.

I filled the gas tank on the engine after the ritual oil-level check. It took four tries at wrapping the cotton rope around the starting ring to turn the engine over with a quick pull before the single spark plug ignited the gasoline vapor and began with its exploding energy to push piston through cylinder, transferring the energy to the v-belt that turned the big flywheel on the Jensen Jack. The head of the jack began thrusting the sucker rod down to fill the pump cylinder with water 975 feet below. Then, on the upstroke, the pump valve in the cylinder closed to force the water into the column pipe for the long upward journey to the waiting storage tank.

While waiting for the water to begin filling the storage tank, I drove the Jeep over to the feed trough to have it ready for the cattle when they arrived. As I grabbed a sack of feed, I happened to look up and see a huge thunderhead, like a tremendous mass of white cotton, coming in low, slipping around the mountain southwest of Samaniego Peak.

I dropped the sack back into the trailer with my eyes fixed on the friendliest cloud I had seen for a year. It moved slowly but steadily on a course that would take it directly over the O Bar J. I stood there entranced, hoping the wind would not decide to come up to scatter and scare away my promising storm cloud. As my cloud slowly wended its way closer, I could see its underside begin to darken, and its entire mass seemed to be spreading—not breaking up but growing outward and upward, heading straight toward the Pacheco pasture. I tingled with anticipation and hope as the cloud approached, still not surrendering its moisture but getting darker and darker.

Impatience prevailed, and I drove up the road to the Middle Tank, keeping a closer watch on the incoming storm than on the narrow ruts through the bleak, drought-stricken landscape. By the time I reached the Middle Tank the cloud was a black, billowing, boiling mass that seemed to cover the entire slope.

The mountains were hidden behind a huge, swirling dust storm sweeping toward me, blocking my view of the cloud so that I could no longer measure its progress. The smell of dust and rain together filled the air, announcing the change from cloud to storm. No scent on earth could have excited me more.

Suddenly the full fury of the wind threw billions of dust and sand particles at the Jeep, whipping through its open sides, stinging my face, and forcing me to close my eyes against the violent onslaught. My eyes were still closed when the first clap of thunder crackled, vibrating the entire landscape with its decibels. I opened my eyes to see the yellow-brown dust fade into black as it moved past my position.

The first thunderclap was followed quickly by another, almost simultaneously with a bolt of lightning that streaked earthward, appearing to ground itself near the Black Dike Mine. The first drops of rain hit the windshield of the Jeep, gathering the surface dust in colloidal droplets.

I scrambled out of the Jeep as I witnessed a wall of rain racing steadily toward me with staccato pelting and pounding on the surface of the droplet-speckled ground. The storm unleashed its full strength and fury. Rain gushed forth as if from a giant faucet suddenly opened, accompanied by billions of volts of electrical energy lighting up the black, nightlike sky and filling the air with its crashing, booming, and echoing. I was experiencing sheer joy—soaked to the skin, water running down my legs into my boots, cold and shivering, not only from being wet but also from feeling the magnitude of the storm.

The earth had cooled and had changed color from the jaundiced tan of desiccation to the rich brown of moisture-filled pores between granules. Soon the surface took on a different texture, a sheen of water as the rate of rainfall exceeded the pull of gravity through the topsoil and collected on the surface. The storm continued unabated, and the excess water began to concentrate into rivulets. Within twenty minutes the rivulets were meeting to form larger rivulets flowing into stream channels, hiding the sand beneath muddy water.

"If this storm continues, maybe the big arroyos will run." I said to myself. I started the Jeep, and drove to the Hall Tank. The storm seemed to subside as I reached the big represo, but there was a puddle in the bottom that had collected from the runoff down the sides of the reservoir. My thoughts jumped to the north pasture, and as I wondered whether headquarters had received any rain, another storm system came in. The downpour commenced again like the second movement of a martial symphony.

The second deluge was quick to collect into rivulets on the saturated surface. I sat in the Jeep, watching and listening, unmindful of my soaked condition. My straw hat was so wet that the brim was beginning to sag over my ears. I speculated how long it would have to rain at the same rate before the big arroyos flooded. It would be rare for the first summer storm to do more than soak the thirsty ground, but this was a rare first summer storm!

The small drainage channels were running about half full. It would take a lot of rain on the mountain before the big arroyo that filled the Hall Tank would run. I dismissed the possibility, trying not to be greedy, trying to be satisfied with the already bountiful storm. I wondered if Chico had been caught out in the deluge, but it seemed more realistic to picture him dry under the barn roof. He had, after all, lived enough summers not to be caught on horseback in the middle of a thunderstorm.

I walked up the ridge that overlooked the Hall Tank and its sand trap to get a better look at the surrounding area. As I reached the top of the ridge, another sound added a new dimension to the thunderclaps and driving rain. I turned toward the low roar coming from the arroyo. Around the bend came a foot-high wall of churning, muddy brown water, swirling swiftly down the channel. The big arroyos had reached flood.

What a sight for me to see! The cleaned out and deepened Hall Tank might fill with precious runoff, a rare runoff from a rare first summer storm. Was this a drought breaker? Would more storms follow to put things back to normal on the O Bar J?

The wall of muddy water hit the sand trap, and for an instant it disappeared into the heavy sand, then it rose quickly to begin spilling out the four-foot-diameter culvert pipe set in the dam of the trap. I trotted down the ridge to watch the runoff enter the represo. Soon the arroyo had brought enough water, and at such a flow rate, that the culvert pipe could barely accommodate the volume. Within minutes the Hall Tank was half full.

The rain eased somewhat, then stopped as quickly as it had begun, but the arroyo continued its flow. I wondered if the other tanks were as fortunate, so I drove toward Pacheco. The sky above was clear, and the sun was breaking through as the storm moved diagonally down and across the bajada. The trees were dripping onto the saturated ground. All I could do was smile.

The rain gauge near the Black Dike measured close to two inches of precipitation. I drove up to look into the tank. In spite of the saturated ground all around, the Pacheco Tank had caught no runoff. The storm center had been farther north and west, but I was too overjoyed at the sight of the wet rangeland to be disappointed at the lack of runoff into Pacheco. I needed feed more than stock water since I could always pump the Pozo Hondo. I turned the Jeep around to hurry back to the Hall Tank. I could see the storm dissipating and judged it to be in the vicinity of Three Points. I wondered if it would last long enough to put water in the bottom of Ray Dill's wheelbarrow. The few times there had been enough rain to measure in the gauges, I would ask Ray how much rainfall he had received. He always measured more than had fallen on the O Bar J, which was considerably higher in elevation than Ray's store. One day after he had given me his measurement I asked him where his rain gauge was located. "I don't have a rain gauge," he said, "I just look and see how much is in the bottom of my wheelbarrow." I didn't bother to comment on the scientific nature of his wheelbarrow, but we continued to exchange rainfall data anyway.

The Hall Tank was full when I arrived. The arroyo had finished draining its watershed, and the water level in the tank was about a foot below the spillway. It looked like a lake! The water in that tank would last two years even if not another drop came down the arroyo in the meantime. I couldn't have been happier driving down the muddy road to headquarters.

Chico was sitting on a bale of hay in the barn. He was slightly damp but smiling so much when he saw me that I thought his upper plate might fall out. He told me he had gotten caught in the storm and that it had rained from headquarters south, missing the cholla country. We both agreed we didn't need to have the cholla any more lively than it was.

A week after the storm there was a green tinge to the range. The cattle scattered in their search for green sprigs long enough to grasp and satisfy their craving. The sky was full of billowy white thunderheads every day for the following two weeks, but none spilled their contents on the western slope of the Sierritas. I watched several storms hover over the Anvil Ranch mountain country. Like most summer convectional systems, these were spotty and localized.

A small shower of twenty-hundredths of an inch fell in the north pasture during the first week in August. The annual grasses in the north pasture had a good start but were showing signs of drying up. The cattle were gaining. The clean white faces made the greening rangeland look more like a cattle operation than it had when it was under the influence of the solemn spell that the bleakness of drought had cast over the land and its occupants. I closed the Middle Tank water lot because the Hall Tank was close enough to serve the animals in that area. The Pozo Hondo still had to be pumped, but not as frequently. The cattle spent less time around the water holes, so their consumption of Paymaster fell somewhat. And I stopped burning cholla! A few cases of screwworm appeared, mostly in calves whose brand scabs were peeling off. Everything seemed to be running smoothly, but there was something about it all that gave me an uneasy feeling that it was all too good to be true. We needed another storm.

The annual grasses started yellowing. When there is an absence of rainstorms at intervals, evaporation into the atmosphere and transpiration by plants consumes soil moisture rapidly, and the vegetation begins to wither from a lack of soil moisture in the root zone. Conditions were all right for the present, but I was concerned about the long term. I needed growth by the perennial grasses to furnish feed during the fall and winter. As long as the short-lived annuals were green, the cattle would concentrate on them, but once the annuals dried up, they would switch to the perennials before these grasses reached their maximum seasonal growth.

During the last days of August the skies were void of storms. Then late one afternoon a few giant thunderheads suddenly came in from the south. I didn't pay much attention to them because they seemed to be moving too fast. I went to bed early.

Toward midnight I was awakened by a thunderclap that sounded as if it was from a lightning bolt in the bedroom. The first was followed by several more, and by the time I had pulled on my boots the rain was pelting the south window of the bedroom. I jammed on my hat and raced for the kitchen to get a better view of the storm. The flashes of lightning made instant daylight out of night, and I could see the barnyard laced with rivulets. I hoped the horses in the corral had not been struck, but I was not about to find out as long as the lightning was prancing around so close.

The storm traveled swiftly to the north. I heard the thunder in the distance as I walked to the corral to check my horses. They were soaked but otherwise all right. They nickered at my approach, so I threw them a midnight snack. The rain gauge showed a half inch. The storm would help the browse, but the annual grasses were too far gone for a comeback. Chico and I rode to the south and Pacheco pastures in the morning and found that the storm had neglected both. It proved to be the last of that summer's storm activity. I began burning cholla again.

Rancho Robles

Robles means oaks in Spanish, but there are no oak trees around Three Points. The ranch was named for the family who established it, and Three Points was first called Robles Junction. Like many formerly large ranches, it had been divided. John Hooperson acquired the north part and successfully began raising crossbred cattle on the floodplain of the Brawley Wash by using a series of spreader dikes to distribute the Brawley's floodwater over an extensive area.

When Jack Stevens came to Tucson, he went to a ranch real estate specialist looking to buy a ranch to get into the cattle business, but he was adamant in his stipulation that the ranch had to have a running stream. Stevens's desire for a running stream had nothing to do with stock water; he wanted the stream to pass through his bar. Jack and his wife Mary included regular drinking in their lifestyle.

The broker, a wily sort, one of those who had given up trying to ranch the O Bar J, showed the south half of Rancho Robles to Stevens on a day when the Brawley Wash was in mild flood. Jack was enchanted, submitted his offer, and the deal quickly went into escrow. By the time Stevens returned to take possession, the Brawley had dried out to its usual bed of sand.

Undaunted, Jack and Mary, a former showgirl in the Bahamas, plunged into the steer business. Of course, every cattle trader in the area wanted a piece of that easy money, and they converged like buzzards on carrion. They had to wait, though, until Jack and Mary built their large pink house with its duck pond in the front yard. Even before the house got underway they changed the name from Rancho Robles to the J Bar M Ranch.

One year in the steer business was enough for Jack. From then on he leased the rangeland to others. The first to lease from Stevens after I arrived in the area was the partnership of George Halloran and John Hooperson. I went down to help them brand, vaccinate, and worm the steers they had purchased. The worming was done orally with capsules containing a compound that would cause the steers to expel any stomach or intestinal parasites they may have been carrying with them from their point of origin. I thought that was a good management practice. They spent the following week helping the steers to get located on their new rangeland.

Jack Stevens had never maintained the dike structures on his part of the old Robles Ranch, but the Brawley Wash did furnish one flood that spread out in spite of the dike system's disrepair. The result was a floodplain covered by *quelite* (careless weed) and Johnson grass. Both plants can cause prussic acid poisoning after they are stressed, by freezing or wilting, for example. Careless weed, in its early growth stages, can cause animals to bloat.

George Halloran arrived at the O Bar J headquarters one summer morning, and as he emerged from his car I could see that something was not exactly right. One shirttail was hanging outside his Levis, and his face showed a look between forlorn and exhausted.

"John, do you have a trocar?" he said. A trocar is an instrument designed to puncture the hide of an animal and penetrate the wall of the rumen, the first large chamber in a cow's stomach. The trocar is hollow so that the gas causing the bloat can escape. The puncture must penetrate somewhat high into the rumen so that any material in there will not plug the inside of the trocar.

"I sure don't, George. What's going on down there?"

"Christ! When I drove up in the pasture this morning, the sky was black with buzzards. Those goddam steers are bloating to beat hell on careless weed. There's five dead already!"

"I've got some tubing. It won't take a minute to make a trocar," I offered.

"Let's try," he said with desperation in his voice. "I have to do something."

We went into the shop, where I found the tubing and cut a section at an angle. I then sharpened it to a knife edge on the grinding wheel. George was on his return trip to his bloating steers in five minutes. Before he was through with the ordeal he had lost a few more steers, but I was glad to hear that the homemade trocar was workable.

When Halloran and Hooperson sold the steers in the fall, I trailered the Paint down to help them gather. Those crossbred steers were not as docile as my Hereford cows, and we had quite a time getting them into the corrals to weigh and ship. The next year the ranch lay vacant. Nobody wanted to lease a range with no feed.

Once the Brawley Wash had been a road, not a large arroyo. It started along the ruts made by wagons on their way to and from Sasabe and Tucson. Early in the century, when the roundup crews of Rancho de la Osa and the Anvil Ranch branded their annual calf crops, there was not enough wood in the Altar Valley for branding fires. They had to heat their irons with fires of cow dung. As the desert grassland ranges deteriorated from overgrazing, suppression of the periodic fire, and other minor factors, brush—including mesquite, catclaw, white thorn, burroweed, and snakeweed—began to invade the rangeland, diminishing the quantity and quality of the grasses. (Actually, burroweed can invade a range even if there is no grazing.)

Grasses have fibrous root systems and are not destroyed by fire, because of the vascular bundle arrangement of their roots, and they help to absorb rainfall gradually into the soil like a sponge. Brush plants, in contrast, have tap root systems and are killed if they are burned by periodic fire while young. Further, while under natural conditions grasses form a homogeneous ground cover, brush plants are more broadly spaced, leaving surface areas exposed and with little or nothing to absorb precipitation. The result is rapid runoff once the top layer of soil becomes saturated. Once this phenomenon had occurred on the slopes of the Altar Valley, the Brawley Wash was born. It followed the ruts of the old wagon road through the center of the valley, and as the erosion continued, it increased the size and depth of the channel.

The neighboring Santa Cruz Valley differed in that the alluvium (the soil washed down from the mountains over geologic time) is much shallower there than in the Altar Valley. The rainfall absorbed by the Altar grassland had a far deeper soil to fill before it became saturated than was the case with the Santa Cruz Valley, where a nearly perennial stream greeted the Spaniards when they arrived with their exotic grazing animals: cattle, horses, sheep, goats, and jackasses. It is easy to blame just one segment of society for what happened to the desert grassland environment, but we need to remember that everyone was ignorant about what would happen to such an ecosystem when these exotic species were introduced and continued to be raised through the many changes in tenure in the area.

John King was the next man to lease from Jack Stevens. The price of weaner calves was low in 1957, so John decided to hold his steer calves over until spring, when he could sell more weight. The Brawley had run slightly a couple of times during the summer, and there was enough forage for the Anvil steers. Since they were native cattle, the risk of their eating the wrong forage at the wrong time was low. Every steer that John put on Rancho Robles lived, grew, and gained weight. I know because I was there to help with the gather.

We made a sweep from the north fence toward the corrals. I was riding the east flank, and the steers were somewhat difficult to start. Just when I thought we had them moving well, five head on my flank broke away from the rest and circled east and north. It was just a matter of my getting around them to chase them back into the herd, but as I rode the Paint at a fast lope over an obscure trail through the brush, he jumped a ditch. We were airborne for maybe a second, but as I looked forward momentarily I saw a coiled diamondback rattlesnake exactly in front of us. The Paint's right forefoot landed directly on the snake's head. I never could tell whether he was even aware of the reptile because we kept on after the steers until we had them turned back. After the steers were safely in the corral, I rode back to see if I could find the snake. It was in the same spot in the trail—dead.

Jack and Mary spent their winters in the Bahamas, mainly because of Jack's inheritance from England, which couldn't be brought into the United States because of tax laws. They always employed a caretaker, not only when they were away but also when they were in residence at the ranch. Bert was one of many. He seemed all right to everyone he met and performed his work well, at least that's what he told everyone around Three Points. When the Stevens couple left for their regular winter sojourn, they left Bert in charge of the ranch with some signed blank checks for paying the monthly utility bills. Jack had not inquired into Bert's past when he hired him; he really had no reason to.

As soon as Jack and Mary left the ranch in Bert's care, he drove Jack's Cadillac to a bar on South Sixth Avenue in Tucson to see his girlfriend. After a weekend of celebrating, they drove back to the Stevens home. But they were not alone in the Cadillac: Bert's girlfriend took her pet monkey with her to her new home at Three Points.

Soon there were several automobiles parked in the barnyard. Over the course of three weeks they would come and go periodically. Nobody in the neighborhood even knew that Jack and Mary had left; they assumed that all the cars parked there meant the Stevens were throwing more of their wild parties. After the signed blank checks ran out, Bert used some other checks he had found in Jack's desk. He just filled them out, expertly signed Jack's name, and cashed them at his favorite bar on South Sixth Avenue. The checks were for an account that had been closed for a year.

Jack had asked a friend from Tucson to check on the ranch occasionally. The friend worked as a car salesman and had sold Jack his Jeep. About three weeks into Bert's extended party, Jack's friend appeared one morning to find Bert and his guests asleep throughout the house. The monkey was the only one awake. It was swinging from drape to drape in the living room, screaming at the intruder. Jack's friend couldn't believe what he was seeing. The drapes were shredded from being used as tree branches by the monkey. The padding from the expensive upholstered furniture was torn and scattered throughout the room, and there was three weeks' evidence that the monkey was not toilet trained.

Jack's friend was at a complete loss to describe the smell of the place when he came to the store and told Ray Dill and me what he had just seen. "I didn't know Jack had left," Ray said and resumed his low whistling.

I heard later that Bert and his entourage, including the monkey, had made a quick exit before the deputy sheriff arrived, but when his check writing was brought to light, Bert was sent back to the Florence prison, where he had already spent several years. Jack returned from the Bahamas the day following his friend's frantic telephone call. I didn't see him; he was too busy getting someone to clean up the results of the monkey. I was at the O Bar J, burning cholla, pumping water, and filling the troughs with Paymaster.

Hutch

The old Western comment "He ain't no cowboy, he just found the hat" could have been applied to Hutch even though he had learned to shape his hat so that it was almost deceiving. I noticed he was still wearing the same hat he had worn to our classes at the university, or one exactly like it. We met by chance one morning and proceeded to the Santa Rita Hotel for lunch.

I learned that since graduating Hutch had been editing bulletins for the extension service, and he was looking for a cattle operation to buy. I never thought of him as having the resources to enter the cattle business, but I had never given it any thought, either. As our conversation continued, he told me that his wife had just come into an inheritance. That made more sense.

I told Hutch that I thought the idea of breaking into the cow business in the middle of a drought was not only risky but also deserving of more thought. I offered to give him a firsthand look at the O Bar J and what I was confronted with. I sensed that Hutch was even more anxious to be in the ranching business than I had been a year and a half before.

Hutch arrived early the following day to accompany me on my daily rounds and see for himself what a drought operation was like. I showed him the cattle, the dry represos, and the way I burned cholla, and I explained the lease I had with Miller. I tried to tell him everything possible to encourage him to wait until the drought was over before investing his wife's inheritance.

I was therefore amazed when we returned to headquarters and he asked if I would be willing to sell him the herd. After a period of silence, I suggested that he bring his wife along the following day to see the ranch. I also told him that I would have a price for the cattle ready for his consideration when he arrived. I emphasized that my price would be well over market because I wouldn't consider selling unless I was at least able to break even. I spent the rest of the day and evening with my pencil until I arrived at prices for the various classes of cattle that would yield a small, almost insignificant, profit for my efforts.

Compared to the cow market at the time, my prices were exorbitant. Still, all I could do was give Hutch my figures and see if his desire to become a cattleman was strong enough to pay for my overpriced cattle. Otherwise I would continue with my stubborn determination to battle the drought, hoping I wouldn't see any more buzzards circling over one of my charges.

Hutch arrived with his wife at midmorning. She wasn't interested in the cattle or even the barn. Her total desire was to scrutinize the house to see if it would be suitable for a woman of her newly acquired means. The major question concerned the workability of the dishwasher in the kitchen. I pleaded ignorance of it, because the only time I had tried to use it I had used laundry soap instead of dishwasher detergent, and the kitchen floor had been flooded with soapsuds.

The price for the cattle I quoted to Hutch didn't seem to make much difference to him. He seemed content that his wife approved of the house. The thought of selling out suddenly became more real to me. I thought he would take more time to consider the transaction. Instead he accepted immediately, contingent, of course, on Miller's agreement to my subleasing the ranch to him. According to my lease with Miller, I had to have his approval to sublease the ranch to anyone, so it was far from a done deal.

"How many cows have horns?" he asked as we walked toward his car.

"Ten, maybe twelve, why?"

"The first thing I'm going to do is round up all those horned cows and dehorn 'em."

"What in hell for?" I asked.

"While I'm brandin' one of their babies, I damn sure don't want one of those horns up my ass," he replied.

I first thought he was joking, but then I realized Hutch was serious. I began to wonder if he had ever been around cattle, except during the lab periods for animal husbandry courses at the university. I introduced him to Joe Miller the next morning at the stockbroker's office, and they made an appointment for lunch a couple of days later. I left it up to them and returned to the O Bar J.

As I went about my work, I reflected on what had been going on with Hutch and wondered about his ability to take care of my cows. I drove to the south pasture to fill feed troughs and pump water. A doe with a young fawn jumped away from the water's edge at the Hall Tank as I drove into the water lot. They raced up the hill, and I marveled at the grace of the doe gliding over the top strand of barbed wire on the fence. I was then startled to see the fawn get one hind leg twisted and stuck between the second and third strands of wire. I walked over there slowly but steadily, talking to the fawn as I approached. Then I reached through the fence and grabbed the leg with my right hand, pulling it toward me to release the tension on the wire. With my left hand I reached for the two twisted strands and spread them apart. With that accomplished, I guided the leg away from the wire and released it.

The doe was at a distance, waiting. The fawn scratched up the gravelly surface of the hill until it reached its mother fifty yards away. Then they both bounded off together. I was glad that all was well with them. As I was filling the feed trough, I wondered what would have been the result if Hutch had been the one to scare the pair off the water.

At the Pozo Hondo I spotted Lucy. I couldn't imagine her without her horns, and the very thought of Hutch dehorning her made me shudder. I thought about the rest—the S Bar S cows. I thought about what would happen to all of my cattle if Hutch became the owner.

He drove out two days later, cold not only toward the thought of taking over the O Bar J and the cattle but also toward getting into the cattle business during the drought. I did not become privy to Miller's conversation with Hutch, but I had a few ideas about what it might have been like.

"I think you made a very smart decision, Hutch, and I'm not the least disappointed," I said. "I kinda like my cows."

I saw Hutch a few years after that. He had a job with a farm and ranch management consulting firm. I couldn't help wondering if his clients dehorned grown cows during droughts to insure against punctured bottoms.

Bull Buying

After Snuffy went under the auctioneer's hammer and burroweed killed another bull, I needed two more sires. Carl Safely had been a professor of animal husbandry at the university but had left to try his hand at earning more money as a livestock consultant and ranch realtor. He had also collected a small number of cattle, which he kept on various ranches. Carl was a proponent of breeding inbred bulls. These bulls were the product of breeding brothers and sisters. When he explained his program to me, I asked him if he was really breeding incest bulls.

My attraction to trying his bulls was more the result of the fact that he was willing to lease them for a hundred dollars a year than it was the inbred genes that Carl said would give their calves hybrid vigor. I understood that hybrid vigor derived from breeding a Brahman animal (*Bos indicus*) to an animal from a European breed (*Bos taurus*), but hybrid vigor from an inbred bull didn't really make much sense to me.

But two of his bulls were located at the San Rafael Cattle Company, and I agreed to look at them.

The trip to the ranch with the RO brand, which had a fine reputation, was a pleasant drive, and I felt good escaping from the O Bar J for a day. I looked at his bulls in the RO corral. They didn't appear to be any different from most bulls. There were some RO bulls in the corral with Carl's. I liked the RO's better. Still, the lease arrangement suited my budget, so I agreed to lease Carl's two inbreds. I also couldn't keep from buying one of the RO bulls for three hundred dollars. He was better than any bull on the O Bar J. As it turned out, I was lucky that I had the RO bull even if it meant I was over the ratio.

A month after Safely delivered the three animals, I noticed that one of the inbreds had no interest in cows in heat. I called Carl to come and get his animals. When he arrived we had a long discussion about his bull's lack of interest in cows. Carl insisted that he had calves from him. "Maybe he just got tired," I said.

Carl was good about returning the lease money I had paid him, and he hauled both inbreds away. The next year I could pick out calves sired by the RO bull by their head shapes, color pattern, and long loins. If it hadn't been for the drought, I would have had an entire bull herd with the RO brand on their left hips. I was lucky to find an alternative.

Pete Perry had managed Rancho Romero, north of Tucson, since I had been the horse wrangler at the neighboring ranch school. I had learned a lot from Pete when I helped with his roundups. Rancho Romero raised registered Hereford cattle, and I was well acquainted with the herd.

I saw Pete at the auction soon after Carl Safely came for his inbreds. In the course of our conversation about market and range conditions, Pete mentioned that he had several bulls left over from the year before and would sell them for two hundred dollars a head. I followed Pete to Rancho Romero from the auction.

The bulls looked good, so I picked out two of them. "When you come for the bulls, you can take that old horse called Apache if you want him," Pete said. "But if you use him much, he'll go poor on you."

"Is he wormy?"

"Hell, I don't know, but you can have him if you want him."

I had known the horse for a number of years, so he must have been more than twenty years old. After thinking about not looking a gift horse in the mouth, I told Pete I would bring my horse trailer when I came for the bulls the following Tuesday.

The bulls located themselves easily, and I considered them excellent additions to increase the quality of the calves. Apache was another story. I gave him a dose of worm medicine the day I unloaded him and another dose two weeks later. He seemed to gain a little weight and looked good. But Pete was right. I rode him once a week but not hard. The old horse went poor, so I took him in to the monthly horse auction. Vernon Mounce bought him for seventy-five dollars.

Not only was my cow:bull ratio good, but the quality of the bull herd assured better and heavier calves. I couldn't see how a bulling O Bar J cow could escape some member of the O Bar J bull fraternity.

Always Something to Do

There is always something to do on a ranch. If it isn't a broken pump, it might be a fence to repair or a first-calf heifer having a difficult time giving birth. My mind was set on dealing with priorities, but there were times when something happened to force me to shift directions. These happenings were always temporary.

John King came by on his way back from town one Saturday to tell me he had a steer and a heifer calf with my earmark in his corral. He couldn't find a brand on either of them, but he said that since they had my earmark I should drop by and determine if they were mine. I drove to the Anvil Ranch the following day.

We entered the large corral and, sure enough, the two animals showed the earmark for the M Flying M, but we couldn't see the brand. I had not used that brand, so the only way they could be my cattle was if they had been part of the Miller calves I had purchased with the rest of the herd. But they were too young to be from that bunch. It didn't make sense.

"Maybe the brands are haired over so we can't make them out," John suggested.

"I don't know," I said. "I can't see how they could be mine from that bunch I bought from Miller. They're too young."

"Let's water them down," John said, and told the two men on horseback to rope and tie the cattle down.

John filled a bucket full of water from the trough, and we proceeded to wet down the hair on the left hip, where the Flying Mustache brand should have been. Neither steer nor heifer showed any brand at all. John said that nevertheless, since they had one of my earmarks, I might as well take them home. "I'll go back and get my trailer," I said.

"It's Sunday," he replied. "They can wait until morning. Come to the house and have a drink."

A drink and conversation with my good neighbor sounded good to me. We sat on the back porch of the old ranch house, talking about a number of subjects. At least an hour had passed when a sudden crack of thunder startled both of us. "I didn't even notice any clouds before we sat down," John said.

"I didn't either."

We left the porch and walked away from the house to see where the storm might be. Another roll of thunder, and the rain descended in sudden sheets. John and I made no move for shelter, we were too busy shouting, "¡Viva la lluvia!" (Long live the rain!). The storm was short-lived, but it dumped thirty-hundredths of an inch while it lasted. I jumped into the Jeep to check the gauge at the Pozo Hondo. I had never covered the distance from the Anvil to my border fence in so short a time. I drove straight to the gauge on one of the fence posts without entering my pasture through the gate. Nothing—not a damned drop! I looked down. The ground was wet right up to the fence line on the Anvil side, but my ground, the width of a single strand of barbed wire away, was bone dry.

Drought can do funny things to one's mind. As I stood

there in awe of the wet Anvil ground next to the still-parched sand of the O Bar J, I wondered if I had done something to deserve this, or was it something I wasn't doing? I had long before decided that organized religions were tax-free businesses that offered something for some people but not for me. I wondered if I was being punished for my belief or disbelief. I must have stood there immobilized by the sight for fifteen minutes before I drove over to the gate to go home.

In the morning I hooked up the trailer to bring the strays to headquarters. I told John about the fence line rain. "Maybe you should start going to church," he said with a laugh.

"Where were you yesterday morning?"

"Feeding cattle at the mountain camp," he replied.

"Yesterday was Sunday. You weren't in church and it rained on you!" I said. We had a good laugh over that one.

The two strays went into the horse corral when I unloaded them. I still didn't think they belonged to me. I explained the situation to one of the brand inspectors, and he said, "Go ahead and brand them if they've got your earmark." I was glad that I didn't.

A week later a couple arrived to look at the strays. I told them that, in spite of their carrying my earmark, I didn't believe the strays were mine. "That's our earmark, too," the man said as we looked at the animals. "They are pretty well haired over. Let's water down the heifer and check her brand."

"John King and I tried that, but go ahead," I said.

We threw and tied the heifer, and the man flipped her over so that her right side was up. I stood there and watched as he watered down the right shoulder. There it was—the couple's brand under the wet hair. "John and I didn't think of them having right-side brands," I said. "Both of our brands are on the left."

I was glad to get rid of the strays to their rightful owners.

The couple ranched east of Tucson but had leased part of a farm bordering the Anvil Ranch near Three Points. The brand inspector had told them about my having a couple of strays.

Lefthand brands are preferable to right because cattle in a corral tend to mill around counterclockwise, and it is easier to check brands if they are facing the person looking at the cattle. But there were so many brands in Arizona registered for the left side that the sanitary board had used up all the possible combinations, at least that was their excuse for issuing only righthand new brands. I told John King about the strays so that if he picked up any more from his north country he would know where they came from.

A month or so before Bridger's roundup, I had just finished nailing a new set of shoes on the Paint and was resting in the shade by the house. The dog jumped up and ran barking to the far side of the corral. Coming down the road from the south pasture was a rider the likes of which I had never seen before. He was almost like an apparition!

The rider was mounted on a dark-brown burro, and his feet were nearly dragging on the ground. The burro traveled with a jog, and his rider rode as if there were no ligaments in his neck or arms. His head wobbled as loosely as his arms, and I wondered how he was able to keep his ancient felt hat from falling off. The two looked like a modern-day Sancho Panza riding his Rocinante, except that the man was gaunt-looking in his dark-brown face and thin of body. As they neared the corrals I wouldn't have been surprised to see a knight looking for a windmill to lance appear at the same time.

The Paint snorted loudly, watching every movement as the odd-looking pair entered the large corral. It was obvious that the man had ridden into the O Bar J corrals before, and from several descriptions I had heard from various neighbors I wasn't surprised when he introduced himself in a squeaky voice as Jorge Moreno.

Jorge lived near one of Carl Bridger's water holes. He was a squatter, but during our conversation he insisted that Carl was his boss. Actually, Carl was stuck with Jorge Moreno, but he supplied him with occasional provisions in return for Jorge's descriptions about how the cattle looked at his rancho. Jorge maintained that he lived on deer and rabbits, but he was thought to enjoy beef on occasion. It was also said that he was prone to acquiring cattle for his patrón.

I wasn't exactly sure how to handle this character. I surely couldn't afford to have him making off with any of my calves, yet I was reluctant to threaten him in any way. I decided the best approach to the situation was to show him the hospitality I would toward anyone, and perhaps during the conversation I would find a way to impress or bluff him into thinking that stealing an O Bar J calf was next to impossible without my discovering it. I also had a strong feeling that Jorge Moreno's reputation may have been based on his hermit lifestyle and strange appearance rather than fact.

Jorge wasted no time in informing me that he had ridden to the O Bar J for food. It seems that Carl had not been to his ranch in some time, and Jorge had run out of staple groceries. As I was searching for a container for some beans, coffee, and potatoes, he pulled an old, tattered flour sack from the pocket of his grimy, ill-fitting pants. I added flour and sugar to the supply before Jorge thanked me and walked to his patiently waiting burro.

The Paint snorted again as the pair passed the horse corral. I couldn't decide whether he was snorting at the sight or the smell. It had probably been at least a decade since Jorge Moreno had given his body the benefit of soap and water. I

saw him once more during Bridger's roundup, but I never discovered any burro tracks in the south or Pacheco pastures,
much as I searched.

When no more rain came after the storm that had filled the
Hall Tank, I had hoped that a winter rainy season would materialize in the fall. The further into fall, however, the bleaker
the prospects seemed. I decided that I should investigate the
possibility of a supplementary income again.

I was slightly acquainted with Carlos Ronstadt, who operated a feedlot on the Agua Linda near Amado, sixty miles
away. I made an appointment with him to discuss employment
possibilities. Carlos was cordial, as usual, and our conversation seemed very productive. He agreed to hire me, and we
were about to get into the question of salary when he asked
how soon I would be able to sell my herd and move to the
Agua Linda.

That stopped me cold. I explained that I did not intend
to sell out and that I would commute, leaving Chico at the
O Bar J to take care of the cattle. I would be able to keep the
troughs full of feed and the water pumped before and after my
workday at Agua Linda.

Carlos stood his ground. I could not have an operation of
my own and be on the Agua Linda payroll. I tried to understand his adamant stand, but I finally realized that the man
didn't have any idea about my stubborn determination to see
the O Bar J cows through the drought. I thanked Carlos for
his consideration and left to pursue other avenues I had been
pondering.

I was, of course, familiar with the way Carl Bridger worked
as an order buyer, operating his ranch as a sideline. I thought
that I could operate the O Bar J and order-buy as a sideline. I had little knowledge of what it would take to break

into that part of the livestock industry, but I believed I could gain a better reputation than most from fair dealing. Naivete strikes again!

Talking with a few order buyers at the auction did not shed much light on the situation. None of them seemed keen on giving a potential competitor much information. However, one of the men I chatted with invited me to his Tucson home to discuss some kind of partnership arrangement he had in mind.

I arrived the following Monday morning. He ushered me into the kitchen and poured two cups of coffee. The preliminary chitchat lasted quite a while. He seemed to be feeling me out for some reason I wasn't aware of. The partner arrangement shocked me considerably.

What this man proposed was that he would get an order from, say, a farmer in Kansas for so many head of steers, heifers, or whatever at a certain price per pound. The next step was to find the kind and number of cattle specified by the order. The farmer in Kansas agreed to pay thirty cents a pound for four-hundred-pound steers, so we would look for four-hundred-pound steers that could be bought for twenty-eight cents. I would then buy the steers for that price. Then my partner would buy the steers from me for thirty cents, as per the order from the Kansas farmer, who would pay my partner two dollars per head as a buying commission. The partnership would then split not only the commission but also the two-dollar-per-hundredweight price spread between what I had bought the steers for, and the thirty cents per pound the farmer had paid my partner for the cattle.

Suppose the farmer had ordered five hundred head of four-hundred-pound steers at thirty cents per pound. That would be $60,000. At twenty-eight cents per pound, the steers would cost $56,000. That's a $4,000 difference. Add a $1,000 buying commission and there would be $5,000 to split between the two partners.

During the entire series of transactions, the farmer in Kansas would think he was paying an order buyer to obtain the best possible deal. That's why he is paying a buying commission. To my way of thinking, the entire scheme was unethical, so I told the man I would think it over. I never called him again. After that experience I decided that the world of cattle buying was a morass of skullduggery that I wanted no part of. I was further determined to work the O Bar J the best I could and forget about trying to increase my cash flow with outside work.

Unchained

Once again the winter rains missed, and the prospect of spring weeds for forage vanished. Would 1958 be another drought year? I wondered again what a normal year would be, if there was anything about the O Bar J that could ever be called normal. Burning cholla, buying Paymaster, and riding over a desiccated range were not the ingredients for any enthusiasm. Even the price of cattle showed no improvement.

My sense of dread about the dry, hot months of May and June was fulfilled once again. San Juan's Day meant nothing, and the Fourth of July was no better. The clouds began to appear around the middle of July, but they were flying so high that there didn't seem to be much reason even to look at them, but every day I looked to see if their flight pattern was lowering.

A week later the storms began. They were spotty, and few dumped their moisture on my side of the valley. It was better than no rain at all, but that was not saying much. I tried to attend the auction every Saturday to keep abreast of the market in case I had to sell off more cows.

One particular Saturday there had been more cattle sold than usual even though the price was about the same for all classes. I decided to leave early and left my seat in the grandstands surrounding the auction ring. As I was walking out of the building toward the parking area, I heard someone call my name. I stopped and turned to see Mike Markoff stepping briskly toward me.

Mike was a real estate broker, the kind who had bought a broad-brimmed hat, a bolo tie, and boots and called himself a ranch specialist. If his boots fit like his hat, he was probably sore-footed. As he approached me he said that he wanted to talk. "Let me buy you a cup of coffee," he said.

I was not anxious to spend any more time in town, but I agreed to sit down with him. He asked if I would list the O Bar J for sale with him. "I don't even own the ranch, Mike," I answered. "All I've got is an option with no money to exercise it."

Markoff quizzed me about the option, and I explained that the price of the ranch depended on fluctuations in the Los Angeles cattle market. The only way I could sell the ranch would be to find a cash buyer, a most distinct improbability.

By the time I stopped for groceries it was midafternoon. The sky was full of thunderheads, and when I had crossed the divide west of Tucson I could see an active storm cell to the south and west. It looked as if I might be getting a good storm for a change, but I wasn't sure. Nevertheless, I pushed down the accelerator, and the pickup speeded up over the Ajo Road. I didn't stop at Three Points, even for the mail, but by the time I turned south, the storm, wherever it had been, was over. Anxious hopes waned as I parked in the barnyard. Not a drop of rain had fallen at headquarters.

I continued to look for moist ground as I drove toward the south pasture. Halfway from the Middle Tank to Pacheco the evidence of recent rainfall was surprising. The trees were still dripping and puddles were everywhere. I pulled up to the Black Dike Mine to check the gauge and couldn't believe the reading of two inches. I stood there in awe of the water level in the plastic device. When I stopped the Jeep at the bottom of the hill next to the Pacheco corral, I heard the frogs and toads! I raced up the road to see over the dam forming the Pacheco Tank, and the full blast of their mating serenade made me shake with joy. Pacheco was full! I looked across the beautiful muddy water and could see where some runoff had flowed over the spillway. After seeing the Pacheco Tank dry for two years, it was a wondrous sight. I looked at the parched bones of the young cow that had become mired shortly before the tank had gone dry and had turned to cracked dried silt. If all I was going to get for summer moisture was a few spotty storms, I was certainly fortunate that the two inches of rain had fallen where it did.

Pumping water would be less crucial with the two reservoirs in the south pasture filled. I walked up the road to see the soaked ground that I could now count on for green perennial growth. Granted, one small corner of the ranch couldn't carry the entire herd, but after such a long dry spell anything looked good to me.

By September the monsoons were no longer bringing moisture from the south, and I was looking forward to another dry winter, but within a week after the end of the thunderheads I noticed the sky change. Frontal systems were beginning to drift in from the west. There was one cyclonic storm that gently sprinkled the entire valley and beyond for a night and a day. If this was the beginning of the winter rainy season, it was early. I couldn't help wondering if it was just another crazy weather pattern that would fail to make any significant contribution to the next spring's feed.

I hadn't given another thought to the conversation with Mike Markoff until he showed up at the ranch headquarters with three men one afternoon as I was getting ready to haul Paymaster to Pacheco. He said he would like to show his clients around, so I told him to help himself. Again, I gave no further thought to Markoff or his clients until Ray Dill told me a week later that Joe Miller wanted me to call.

Miller's maid ushered me into Joe's office, and I sat down in the familiar leather-upholstered chair to wait for my landlord to appear. He greeted me with a handshake and a scowl interrupted by a forced smile that faded quickly into the scowl again. I hadn't the slightest idea what was on the man's mind. "I understand you have some sort of trade deal going on the ranch," he said. "I ran into Mike Markoff the other day."

It was clear as a bell why Joe had left his message with Ray Dill. I didn't know that Markoff and Miller were even acquainted. I had to think fast. "Hell, Joe, I don't know if anything will come of it, but I'm open to it if it's right," I said.

"John, I really don't want to sell the ranch. I bought it for a land investment, and I'm really not ready tax-wise to sell it now."

"I've been doing a lot of thinking about my situation out there," I said, "and I've analyzed the capacity of the ranch very closely. There doesn't seem to be any way I can come out on it because I think that one hundred and fifty cows is all the ranch will carry. And one hundred and fifty cows are not going to have enough calves to pay all the expenses plus my own living. You know as well as I do that the only escape I have from that ten-year lease is to exercise my option to buy the ranch. You also know that I have to come up with the cash because there is nothing in the option specifying any type of financing. Therefore, Joe, I have to find someone who will buy from me before I can exercise the option."

I didn't mention Markoff and his clients. I didn't have the slightest notion of what was going on in that arena. All I knew for sure was that I had to stay on my toes with that conversation.

"What will you take, right here and now, for your option, John?"

I wasn't prepared for the blunt challenge. I would have preferred more time to feel out the situation, more time for hemming and hawing.

"Joe," I said finally, leaning toward him and looking him straight in the eye. "I'll take an escape clause written into the lease, the rent I am now paying for the remainder of the lease, and permanent possession of the O Bar J brand."

"How about a six-month notice on the escape clause?" he asked.

"Fine," I replied without any hesitation.

"All right, John," he said, no longer scowling. "Consider it done. I'll have my attorney draw up the necessary papers."

I left the Miller mansion with a newfound sense of accomplishment. I now had a lease that would allow me the flexibility I needed to make the O Bar J pay. If it wouldn't pay, I could leave. In those few moments sitting in Miller's office I had cast off the chains of that ten-year lease.

Another cyclonic system rolled in the following day. From past sad experience I knew I couldn't depend on winter rains to bring spring feed, so I thought long about what to do about the present and future management of my cows.

I had heard that a farmer north of Tucson, near Marana, had some milo maize sorghum stubble and cotton stalks available for pasture. I drove out to look at the situation. The stubble was the remnants of his sorghum crop after he had cut it for ensilage, and there were plenty of weeds and Johnson grass in the field of harvested cotton. The price was two dollars per head per month. The farmer furnished the salt and water. I made certain that my cattle would be the only ones on the fields.

Chico and I rode for three days, gathering fifteen of the oldest cows to ship to Marana. Crooked Horns was one of them. I didn't go with the shipment because I had decided to cull the herd to 150 cows, and we continued our gathering until the cattle I wanted to sell were all in the north pasture. The keepers were given the best of the O Bar J range for the winter.

The livestock auction had an occasional bargain. On the first Saturday in October I arrived an hour before the sale was due to begin and wandered through the alleys, looking at the various pens of cattle to be sold. One corral held eighteen Mexican steers that were every possible color. Several were straight Brahman Humpies, so called for the large hump at their withers. It was not a uniform pen of steers to be sure, and I wondered why there was only one lot number pasted to the back of only one of the steers. It seemed more logical to send them through the sale ring separately.

I sat down in the sale barn when the auction began to watch the price of cows so I could figure what my thirty-five culls in the north pasture would be worth. There seemed to be a lack of interest in the bidding, and some of the regular buyers began to drift out to the coffee shop before all the cattle had been sold. The auctioneer seemed perturbed. Hereford steers were bringing twenty to twenty-three cents a pound. Crossbreeds were selling for eighteen to twenty cents a pound. Cows like mine were bringing between 115 and 125 dollars a head. I always figured cows by the head.

By the time the Mexican steers were driven into the ring, the two buyers who had been bidding on most of the cross-bred cattle were drinking coffee in the sale barn's restaurant. The auctioneer started them at eighteen cents a pound but couldn't find a bidder. He tried sixteen, still with no success. I began to wonder if there was something about the steers that I had not noticed out in the pen. I had spotted some that were still bulls.

Finally the auctioneer tried the steers at thirteen cents a pound and got a bid from a farmer-looking fellow who had not budged all morning. I nodded my head cautiously at thirteen and a quarter. The farmer reluctantly bid thirteen and a half. The auctioneer then tried for fourteen cents, looking at me and somewhere else, trying to make me think there was a third party interested in the steers. I nodded at the fourteen cents. The farmer shook his head. Down came the hammer, and I had bought my first bunch of Mexican steers. They were far from the best-looking pen of cattle I had ever seen, but I hadn't bought them for their beauty. For fourteen cents a pound I had a group of big-framed steers who would think they had been sent to heaven when they saw the O Bar J and compared it to their home range in Mexico.

The steers weighed an average of 405 pounds. I arranged for their delivery to the ranch, but before going home I bought some worming capsules to give them a good start. I had a touch of buyer's remorse on the way back to the ranch. I wasn't sure about adding eighteen steers to the ranch when I had no idea what the spring feed conditions would be. I would have been more comfortable to wait, but if I had hesitated I would probably have had to pay far more than fourteen cents a pound. I had gambled. Buying and selling steers is always a gamble because when a steer is ready to sell, you have to sell him regardless of the price. Steers can't give birth to calves.

My new hand of poker arrived late Sunday afternoon, and I walked through them in the corral to get further acquainted with them. I was glad to see they were gentle, not snortin' wild like a lot of Brahmans such as Ranger once raised on the Gunsight Ranch. I threw some hay into the feed bunks for them as Chico rode in to unsaddle. He was surprised to see the steers in the corral. He didn't say anything as he looked them over. I could see he was acquainting himself with them. "They were a *ganga*," I said, a bit sheepishly.

"We'll see if they are bargains when you sell them," he said.

We branded and wormed the steers the next day. Five were bulls, so we castrated them. They drifted out of the gate into the north pasture. I was not sure about what I had accomplished.

I told John King about my purchase so that if any strayed into the Anvil range he wouldn't be surprised to see the O Bar J on a Mexican steer. John was still pessimistic about spring feed prospects and added that he would stick to his Hereford cows. "No crossbreed will ever eat Anvil grass as long as I'm here." That didn't make me feel any better about my steer gamble.

Two weeks later I saw one of the steers, a lanky brindle with stubby horns, grazing next to the Sasabe Road. Chico went down to bring him back as I rode the north boundary fence to find out where the steer had escaped. I picked up his tracks along the fence and followed them. I had long before learned that tracks can reveal a lot of things. I could even tell when a strange vehicle had entered the ranch, and if it was still there.

The brindle's tracks stopped in a confusing pattern. I

looked at the fence and saw a patch of brindle hair caught on one of the barbs in the wire. Looking over on the Anvil side I saw where the devil had landed. A fence jumper—that was one thing I didn't need to contend with.

We drove the brindle to the south part of the pasture, hoping he would get himself located there and be content enough not to jump any more fences. I knew that plan had failed when John King told me he had one of my Mexican steers in his headquarters corral. I hitched up the horse trailer and sure enough, just as I suspected, the brindle steer was there waiting for me. This time I decided to keep him in the headquarters corral and feed him from the Bermuda grass straw I had stacked outside the barn. The price of hay had risen so much after the drought relief program started that I had bought a truckload of Bermuda straw for half the price of alfalfa hay. It wasn't very palatable for horses, but it would do for cattle, especially the brindle fence-jumper from Mexico.

Lookin' Better

The winter rainy season continued. My hopes for spring feed on the ranch were boosted with every frontal system that arrived. Since the sparse and spotty summer rains had kind of melted into the cyclones from the Pacific, I had had my doubts that the storms would continue through the winter.

I saw George Halloran one day in late December. "How are things going at the ranch?" he asked.

"Lookin' better," I replied. "I'm still feeding supplement, but I quit burnin' damn cholla. The browse is staying green, and I'm only pumping the deep well every fourth day."

"How do the cows look?"

"They're holdin' up fine, and it looks like I'll have a good calf crop."

"I leased a small place out Sahuarita way," he continued. "You don't know where I could find some decent cows, do you?"

"I have thirty-five head of really nice cows I'd sell," I said. "Come out and look at them if you want. I'm cutting my herd of mother cows down to a hundred and fifty. I already sent the old cows to stubble in Marana."

"Suppose I come out day after tomorrow?"

"Sounds good to me, George," I said. "If you get there around ten in the morning, most of them ought to be in for water and you can get a good look at them."

He didn't ask me about price, and I didn't volunteer. I was happy that I could try to feel him out as he looked at the cows. I knew that cow prices had improved quite a lot since I had decided to cut my numbers, enough so that I would be selling the old cows from Marana the following week.

Chico and I rode out early on the morning George was due to look at the cows, and by nine thirty all of them were in the trap at headquarters. He was on time, and I walked with him into the trap. About half the cows had calves by their sides. "The others look bred to me," George said as we walked slowly around the cattle.

"I can see several pretty heavy ones that should calve any day," I added.

"Well, John, I like the cows," he pronounced. "How much are you asking?"

"One sixty, pairs or singles," I said firmly.

"Well, I can never give someone their asking price," he replied. "I'll give you one fifty-five."

"You just bought yourself thirty-five cows, George!"

He walked to his car and opened his checkbook on the hood. "If you can keep these cows up until tomorrow, I'll send a truck for them," he said.

"That will be fine, George, but what about the brand inspection?"

"Damn, I forgot about that. I'll call tonight and see if I can get one of them to come out in the morning," he replied.

"All I have to feed them is that sorry Bermuda straw."

The brand inspector arrived early, and we had already put

them in the corrals. George arrived just as the inspector was filling out the inspection papers. The truck was an hour behind him. While we waited for the truck, the Mexican steers came in for water. I had latched the gate to keep the cows in, so the steers waited outside. I drove a few cows out of the big corral into the two other pens, then I opened the gate for the steers. They trotted up to the long water trough. "Those are good-looking steers, John," Halloran remarked.

"They're not doing too badly," I replied.

"Do you want to sell them?"

"Not right now," I said. "I'm figuring to sell them in May. That is, if the rain keeps up and I get some spring weeds. I've got about thirty of my Hereford steers to sell then too."

"Would you be willing to contract them to me now?"

"Depends on what you'll pay, George."

"How much will they weigh?" he asked.

"I'd say that will depend on what kind of feed, if any, might come on this spring," I replied.

George went back to the fence to look at the Mexican steers again. I was wondering what was going through his head. I also had only a vague idea about what price I should ask on a contract for such a faraway date. George solved the last problem for me.

"I'll tell you what, John. I'll give you twenty-four for the crossbreeds and twenty-eight for the Herefords."

I paused a few moments, for effect more than anything else. "George, I never sell to someone for what they bid." We both grinned. "I'll take twenty-four and a half for the crossbreed, and twenty-nine for the Herefords, weighed off the trucks at the auction, no pencil shrink, and you pay the trucks. May 1 delivery."

"You just sold your steers, John," he said as he continued to grin.

We went to the kitchen to fill out the contract for the

steers. George wrote a check for the two-thousand-dollar deposit and handed it to me. The truck rumbled into the barnyard and backed up to the loading chute.

I told Chico about contracting the steers. "¿Ganga o no ganga?" I chided. A happy smile spread over his face, and he gave me a pat on my arm.

Two days later I was at the auction, watching my old cows from Marana go through the ring. One had died, so there were fourteen left to be sold. The price for canner cows was holding well because the greyhound racing season in Tucson was in full swing. One slaughterhouse was doing a brisk business boning out old cows and selling the meat to the dog racers. Crooked Horns came snorting into the ring, stopped short, and looked around with her one eye. I nudged a friend of mine sitting next to me. "There goes the best goddam cow that ever made a living on the O Bar J." Before jumping onto the scales, old one-eyed Crooked Horns charged the ring man, forcing him to seek shelter behind a shield built into the ring.

The temperature had dropped overnight as one more winter storm system moved in. Just before sunrise I opened my eyes to find two inches of snow on the desert outside my bedroom window. The large white flakes were still falling gently from the sky. I dressed quickly and walked out into the white-blanketed barnyard. The fence posts wore tufted white hats, and the tops of tree branches were all covered by ridges of white. The strangest sight was the cholla spines all trimmed with snow. The entire desert scene was like an eerie fantasy with a dead-still silence as the flakes fell noiselessly earthward.

As I walked down the road toward the bunkhouse I looked back to see my boot tracks where they had broken the blanket of white. Chico's strong brew contrasted beautifully with the chill in the air. He seemed more pensive than usual, and I wondered if the snow had anything to do with his mood.

I watched through the window as the snowflakes gradually stopped, signaling the end of the storm. We had said all there was to say about the snow. Then the old vaquero told me what was on his mind.

He said he realized that I could handle all the work on the ranch and that he knew I was concerned about the financial situation caused by the drought. He then offered to work for me for no wage. "Just bring me some beans and flour once in a while," he said.

His generous offer was one of the finest compliments ever paid me. I quickly dismissed the idea, although I told him that I was very grateful for his concern and understanding. I told him further that I sincerely needed him, that his care of the cattle was essential to the O Bar J. I was glad that I really did want and need him because he would have known in an instant if I was not being truthful.

The snow had melted by noon.

The Spring of
Fifty-Nine

Toward late January it seemed as if spring was trying to arrive early. The daytime and night-time temperatures were on an equal rise. By the first week of February, the weeds were beginning to push their first leaves out of the ground. They were slow at first, almost cautious, but by Lincoln's Birthday the desert was green and the cattle were scoured, their hind legs splattered with green manure. The storms continued almost on a weekly schedule. The rising cattle prices reflected the excellent range conditions throughout the Southwest. The conversations among cattlemen attending the auctions were optimistic for the first time in three years, but there were also lingering questions: Had the drought really broken, and what about the coming summer?

It was a joy to ride through the pastures and see cattle filling out, slickin' off, and licking their sides. The Mexican steers were growing. I had turned the brindle fence-jumper loose when the weeds had made a good start. He stayed in the north pasture and thrived. My supply of Paymaster had dwindled to a small stack in the barn, but I didn't order another load. I wanted to wait to see what May and June would bring. I wished I had a hundred fourteen-cent Mexican steers to use up the surplus weed crop while it was green.

The first Saturday of March I stopped at the auction to see what the market was doing, more out of curiosity than anything else since I had sold everything I intended to sell.

A cotton farmer from Marana with whom I was slightly acquainted approached me in the sale barn. "John, would you happen to know where I could find a good herd of Hereford cows?" he asked. "I'm wantin' to ease out of cotton and get into cattle."

"How many are you looking for?" I inquired.

"I've got room for about a hundred and fifty right now, with all these weeds and my stubble," he said. "Once my perma- nent pasture gets started, I should be able to run around three hundred, I figure."

My mind sprang into action immediately, and I decided to show him my cows. I gave him directions to the O Bar J and made an appointment for him to look at the cattle the following Monday.

During the drive back to the ranch I was somewhat as- tounded at what had just transpired. Sleep was impossible that night, so I went out to the Jeep and drove all over the ranch, mulling over in my mind the decision I faced.

Once I priced the cattle, I would have to sell if the farmer agreed. That would be followed by using my escape clause to cancel the lease. I would then be out of the cow business unless I found somewhere else to go and then bought another bunch of cows to husband. With the high price of cattle, I would have to wait until the market dropped substantially be- fore buying in again. My experience with the O Bar J had shown me that with my limited capital I would only be capable of a small cow-and-calf operation. With such limitations, my annual income during normal years would be a small amount of interest on my investment. Therefore, I would have to keep repeating what I had done on the O Bar J—that is, buy in on a low market and then wait out and fight my way through another drought until I could sell high. I was not sure that I wanted to take those risks again. Another incentive for me to sell out was that in spite of the bountiful weed crop, May and June would burn it all off, and what if there were no summer rains?

By Sunday evening I had pursued every economic thread of the cattle business. I went to bed exhausted from the mental gymnastics. I had determined to sell the cattle for top dollar to the cotton farmer, who seemed overanxious to be a cattleman.

It took all morning to drive my buyer around the ranch. The cattle looked beautiful grazing on the green carpet of weeds. I explained how deeply I had recently culled, so it was a far younger herd than he could hope to find elsewhere. I pointed out the steer calves that were contracted to Halloran so that he could see the quality he could expect from the cows and bulls. I was careful not to oversell the cattle because I didn't want to scare him away from the deal. I figured the most effective procedure would be to show him what I had, let him ask me for a price, and then let him go home to think about it.

Everything went smoothly. I could feel that he liked the herd. He didn't hesitate to ask my prices. I priced the cows at $230, the bulls at $450, and the replacement heifer calves at $150. The farmer didn't seem to flinch at my prices, and I made an appointment to see him in the evening two days later.

I received a cordial welcome from the farmer and his wife at their Marana cotton farm. I had arrived at eight o'clock in the evening, hoping the late hour would spur him to a quick decision, but it was soon evident that I was with a man who needed to be sold.

I walked out the door at two thirty in the morning with a sizable bank draft in my pocket. I had sold the herd. I stopped at an all-night truck stop on the outskirts of Tucson and sat down at the counter for some much-needed coffee. I was happy with the prices we had agreed on: cows, $225; bulls, $400; and the replacement heifers at $125. The price for the heifers was how I had sweetened the deal. I was definitely receiving top dollar for my cattle. Delivery was in ten days.

As I drove home in the early morning, I felt good about my decision to sell. I would no longer have to wonder about rainy seasons, track the clouds, or follow a flock of buzzards circling in the sky to see if one of my animals was lying dead on the range. True, I would no longer experience the exhilaration at seeing the Hall Tank fill with runoff and hearing the frogs and toads chirping in their mating ritual. But I had no regrets. The world was open to me; like the brindle steer, I had found a place in the fence to jump over.

Chico's future presented a concern. He was happy that I had done so well in the sale of the herd, but we both knew that after the steers were shipped on May 1 there would be no more work on the O Bar J for either of us. I went to the Anvil to tell John King the news and ask him if he would hire my friend. John agreed that Chico would be an asset to the Anvil. Chico seemed content and thanked me for my efforts on his behalf.

The only sadness I felt was that after the steers were gone I would no longer be working with Chico and that John King would no longer be my neighbor. I had formed strong friendships with both men.

The process of gathering the cattle began with closing the gates to all the water holes in the south and Pacheco pastures. We rode every day, moving all the cattle into the north pasture. Then we trapped the steers as they wandered in for water at headquarters and drove them all to the south pasture to keep them separate from the herd. The day before my delivery date, John King came up to help us gather the north pasture.

The cattle were grazing the lush spring feed in the early morning. We spread out to start a sweeping drive to the corrals. After the first and major drive, we made another sweep of the two sections west of headquarters. The roundup was finished by noon. Chico and I rode cleanup during the afternoon and found that the morning's work had brought everything in. I threw a few bales of hay into the holding trap where the cattle would remain overnight, the last night there for many that had been dropped as newborn calves on the O Bar J range.

As I walked slowly among the cattle, I thought about the ones that were no longer members of my herd: Bones; Crooked Horns; Snuffy Smith, the prickly pear addict, and his christening of the white Ford's hood; the dead ones, bleached bones parched by desert sun. I felt a lot of respect for these animals and hoped that the cotton farmer from Marana knew enough about cattle to take care of the herd he was going to haul away.

The following day the early-morning air was crisp as we rode through the holding trap, cutting out the replacement heifers first and then the bulls. One cow had calved during the night, and two others looked like they were close to their times. The cotton farmer brought two sons to help with the loading. One of them had driven a bobtail truck. I explained my plan for tallying and loading the cattle, which included separating the small calves to avoid in-transit injuries. My advice included using their bobtail truck to haul the cow with the newborn calf and the other two cows that were close to calving. The cattle were mine until they stepped into the trucks from the loading chute.

When the first of the cattle trucks labored up the road to receive its load, the brand inspector was in the corral with the heifers, checking their brands. I positioned myself on the chute fence along with the farmer to tally the cattle as they were loaded. I didn't know how much the farmer's sons knew about working cattle, so I told them to work them easily and slow because they weren't heading for any scales. The heifers were first up the chute, then the bulls. By the time the heifers were loaded, the other trucks had arrived and were waiting in the barnyard.

Chico and I rode out into the trap and drove all the cows and calves into the corrals. I told him to try to segregate the three cows and the baby calf for the bobtail. As those familiar white-haired faces walked up the loading chute, I couldn't resist the temptation to reach down and touch a few special matrons like Lucy. We had paneled off all the young calves in the front part of one semi's trailer. By noon the O Bar J herd was starting its journey down the road to Marana.

The cotton farmer and I took our tally sheets to the kitchen and totaled all the different cattle, and I put the bank draft into my pocket. "I reckon I'm out of the cow business now," I said. "They're your cows now. Be good to them, and they'll be good to you."

I walked out into the corrals with an empty feeling, but I also felt a sense of accomplishment at having husbanded that herd through three years when the odds for survival had been slim. In the long run I had made good money by selling at top prices. I still had the steers to deliver in May, but I wondered if I would ever again own a cow herd. I put the letter I had written to Joe Miller canceling the lease in my pocket along with the bank draft and drove into town.

Que le Vaya Bien

C hico helped the Anvil crew with their roundup for a few days. It was a good opportunity for him to see how John King operated. Then he returned to look after the steers that were flourishing on the abundance of spring forage.

One morning, as usual, I went down to the bunkhouse to join him in morning conversation and found him still in his bed, unable to rise. It was obvious that the old cowboy was in pain. I asked him if he had fallen or hurt himself in some way. He replied in the negative, but he declined to go into any detail. He asked to be taken into town to his daughter's house.

I was worried when I went back for the pickup truck. I lifted Chico from the bed and carried him to the cab, where I propped him up as best I could. When we reached the highway, I drove faster than my usual speed. His daughter helped me to get him into her house, and I gave her the telephone number of the Three Points Store in case she needed me for anything. I promised to be back in a couple of days to see how my friend was getting along.

The following morning I telephoned and was disturbed to hear that Chico had been admitted to the hospital. I went directly to see him. The pain was gone from his eyes, and he was able to tell me that his doctor was planning to operate on him the next morning. While we were chatting, the doctor came into the room. I inquired about Chico's condition and was stunned to learn that the surgery was to remove his cancerous colon. There was also the possibility that the cancer had spread elsewhere. I told my friend that I would return the next day to see how he was getting along, trying not to sound concerned. The old cowboy was not easily fooled and told me not to worry, that he would be up and around to help me gather the steers and ship them.

There was hope, but I cried halfway back to the ranch just remembering how he looked so out of place lying in the hospital bed covered by a green smock instead of mounted on the Paint ready to ride the circles.

I telephoned the doctor the next afternoon. He seemed satisfied with the operation but told me to postpone any visits for a day because Chico was still under sedation. I drove in to see him the next evening. Considering what he had been through, he looked amazingly well, and my hopes grew for his recovery. I visited the hospital every other evening for ten days. Just before he was due for discharge, I walked into his room and I could see that my friend was upset.

He told me that the head administrator had brought an interpreter to his room to demand that he pay the hospital bill. The idea of this person upsetting him and perhaps impairing his recovery angered me. I told Chico not to worry about the bill because I would "bail him out." Then I went to the business office and informed the director, "Francisco Leyvas is my responsibility, so don't be around bothering him."

During my next visit, Chico was chuckling as he related how he had sent a friend to sign for him at the bank and withdraw money from his savings. Chico had placed the twenty-five hundred dollars on the table next to the bed and called for the director. When she arrived with her interpreter, Chico, sitting upright and looking straight ahead, said one sentence, "Here is your money," followed by a few well-chosen Spanish epithets. I would have enjoyed being present to hear how close an interpretation was given to the dunning director.

I visited the nursing home as much as possible, but it pained me deeply to watch his decline. When I heard about Chico's death, I had already done the crying. I didn't attend the funeral. For me Francisco Leyvas died when he unsaddled the Paint for the last time. The last of the fast reata men was gone, not killed by a wild mountain steer but wasted to nothing. Que le vaya bien, vaquero viejo. Go with love, old cowboy.

Adiós

I liked George Halloran. From my experience I thought of him as an honest man. After mailing the registered letter to Joe Miller canceling the lease, I contacted George to tell him that if he was interested in leasing the O Bar J, I would do whatever I could to help.

The first step was to show him around the ranch, and while I was doing that I explained all the details of the lease I had signed with Miller. I also tried to point out some of the pitfalls George might expect. He was interested enough to meet Joe Miller, so I introduced them to each other. From there the chips had to fall wherever they might. I didn't inquire about the particulars when George came out to tell me he had signed a lease with Joe Miller.

"When do you start, George?" I asked.

"The first of May, after we weigh the steers I bought from you," he said.

It was good news for me. I could leave the ranch before the six months were over.

The cyclonic systems had dwindled and quit. The April had sun dried the weeds to powder, but the steers were doing well. I drifted them gradually into the north pasture and by mid-April had decided to lock them in the headquarters corral to feed them what remained of the Bermuda straw. The Paymaster was gone. I was happy not to have the prospect of shouldering any more twenty-ton loads of hundred-pound sacks from the semi into the barn.

Since all the steers were safely penned in the corrals, I didn't need to keep the horses around. John King bought the two duns, but I gave him the Paint. I had planned to give the Paint to Chico.

It felt strange that all I had to do was throw the Bermuda straw out in the big corral every morning and evening, feeding the steers on the ground. The O Bar J range was empty of cattle for the first time in many years, perhaps since the thirties.

Early on the morning of May 1, George Halloran, the brand inspector, and the two trucks I had ordered arrived to receive the steers. We separated the Mexican steers from the Herefords to facilitate the weighing process once they reached the auction.

George and I were both surprised at the appearance of the steers after unloading. Cattle will generally shrink during transit, but these steers had been jostled around in the trucks for almost forty miles, and they looked as full as when they'd walked up my loading chute. I motioned to the yard hands to start weighing. The average weight of the Herefords was 428 pounds, the best I had ever shipped from the O Bar J—proof to me that my management had been going in the right direction. The Mexican steers astounded me by averaging 615 pounds. My gamble had paid off in jackpot dimensions!

I walked out to the loading chute after returning from town, my ceremony of good-bye before loading up the last of my gear. As I leaned against the chute, wondering if I would ever again ship cattle, I noticed solid masses of manure on the ramp. When cattle are being loaded, they tend to become loose-boweled. I was so intrigued that I picked up a stick to investigate the odd phenomenon further. There were small pebbles and sand throughout the mass, appearing to be mortared together, forming a bovine adobe. I had shipped a bunch of constipated steers. Because I had fed the steers on the ground instead of from a trough, they had ingested the sand and pebbles along with the dry Bermuda straw. I had not only sold the steers for a decent price, I had discovered a preventative measure for shrink.

In Retrospect

The drought of the fifties was the worst drought in southern Arizona in four hundred years. To survive the drought with a cow-and-calf operation, I had learned persistence and determination combined with an ability to be flexible. Dreams are fine. I fulfilled mine of becoming a cowman. I realized the accomplishment, and I knew when the dream was over. The drought years of the fifties were good years for the buzzards, and they turned out to be good years, too, for the kid from New York, who had once thought cowboys wore nothing under their chaps but their bare bottoms.

The drought of the fifties instilled self-confidence in me. Since then I have never been afraid to change directions in my life. The word *career* is missing from my personal vocabulary because it has the connotation of forever, and I don't want forever. Suppose I tire of doing something? Then I want to be able to think of something different to do.

I also experienced joy and beauty on the western bajada of the Sierrita Mountains during the drought of the fifties. Looking across the Altar Valley at beautiful sunsets over the chain of mountains to the west and enjoying sunrises over Samaniego Peak to the east were always a joy in spite of the constant dilemma of the drought. Watching the baby calves arrive and bounce along beside their mothers gave me a thrill every time. I experienced the beauty of trust between friends, and the caution needed when dealing with those who would always be strangers. There was, of course, a feeling of ecstasy after the drought relinquished a storm for the O Bar J. It was a unique time for me.

After I loaded those last steers from the O Bar J headquarters, I spent a few years buying Mexican steers and raising quarter horses. I then decided to return to graduate school and pursue an advanced degree in geography in order to teach at the university level. I wrote a master's thesis on drought and read all I could find about the fire ecology of grasslands.

The southeastern part of the O Bar J range, so crucial to the maintenance of my cow herd during those drought years, is on the fringe of what was once called desert grassland. The grassland was kept a grassland by fire. Without fire every few years, brushlike mesquite, catclaw, burroweed, and snakeweed will invade the grassland. As the brush increases, the grasses diminish in quantity as well as quality. Eventually the personality of the landscape becomes brushland instead of grassland. It is possible that my friend, the low-growing shrub *guajilla,* could be considered one of the invaders.

Overgrazing has been blamed for a myriad of conditions, past and present, including the invasion of brush into the desert grassland. It is easy to place the blame on early ranchers, but they were raising livestock not only before the fragile nature of grasslands was known but also before *ecology* was even a word in our language. In any case, overgrazing was not the only culprit. Periods of extended drought like the fifties, animals and birds spreading seeds from the trees and shrubs, and climatic changes have been suggested as parts of the story.

The brush invasion had begun long before I bought Joe Miller's herd, but the perennial grasses and guajilla were still in good enough shape to provide a substantial hole card of feed on that southeastern part of the ranch when I found it necessary to burn cholla for the cattle located in the north pasture. The brush provided browse for the O Bar J cattle when the lack of rain frustrated the growth of the grasses.

The two deep wells on the O Bar J were major factors in allowing my persistence to survive the drought of the fifties. Had I been cattle ranching there during the drought of the thirties, before water-well and pump technology had evolved, there is no question that I would have been forced to sell out along with Ranger and Bud Schmeiding.

The drought of the fifties had a serious economic impact on the ranching industry in the Southwest. It would have affected urban areas to a greater extent (as the drought of the thirties had) if there had not been a migration to Southwestern cities, creating a favorable economy.

Cattle raising has been part of the Southwestern culture for two hundred years. It has been romanticized completely out of proportion by the motion picture industry and others. The ranching industry has become a haven for tax write-offs for those in positions of wealth, and in most cases the husbanding of cattle is secondary to real estate investment and land speculation. The drought of the fifties seemed to accelerate that trend as many legitimate cowmen were forced, or lured, to sell out. The ranching community is correct, however, in maintaining that theirs is a way of life unique to the West, and the investment in land and livestock is considerable. However, the deterioration of grassland watersheds is attracting more and more attention, along with other environmental issues. At one time in the history of Arizona, cattlemen had greater political power than urban or mining interests. Today there is, on the one hand, a cry from environmentalists to raise grazing fees, or even to eliminate cattle raising, on the public lands. On the other hand, there is the stubborn resistance of ranchers trying to maintain their way of life. There is validity in both arguments, so the search for a solution to the dilemma has become mired in emotion.

After thirty-three years, I returned to the O Bar J to find the north pasture subdivided, with houses scattered around a grid of streets where the O Bar J cows once struggled valiantly to survive the drought of the fifties. Perhaps the current use of that pasture is more appropriate than cattle raising. The south pasture, which I considered the best part of the ranch, has been further invaded by shrubs and trees, with very little of the black grama and other perennial grasses in evidence. The mesquite, catclaw, white thorn, desert hackberry, and Jerusalem thorn are larger and denser than when I was riding the Paint to check my cattle. Perhaps the guajilla that once provided me with a hole card in the southeastern part of the ranch is difficult to find, not only because of grazing but also from drought kill. Certainly pine in New Mexico and mesquite and creosote bush in the Pinacate region west of the Altar Valley suffered drought kill during the drought of the fifties.

Burroweed and snakeweed seem to have replaced much of the grass that the ranch supported in the fifties. These two invaders germinate in the spring, especially after copious winter rains. During the spring of 1993 the south pasture was almost carpeted with burroweed and snakeweed seedlings. The arroyos are wider, some are deeper. Most of the roads I used to travel are now arroyos. Two rusted pipes protrude from the middle of a widened arroyo where the Middle Tank once furnished water to my cows when the Hall Tank was dry. The sole remnant of the corral I built at the Middle Tank is a piece of rusty barbed wire I once installed as part of a corner brace for the corral.

The Hall Tank has been enlarged considerably, but the sand trap appears to have washed out to the south. The Pacheco Tank has also been enlarged. The Pacheco well is still where it was thirty-three years ago, but there is no evidence that it has been pumped for many years. The Pozo Hondo looks almost the same. The storage tank is still used to store the precious water pumped by the old Jensen Jack, but the pipeline is mostly a rusty remnant. The water lot looks much the same, but extensive working corrals have been built on the side of the fence where it rained on the Anvil Ranch during that particular storm when not one drop landed on the O Bar J side.

After the drought of the fifties ended, I had decided that the fourteen sections of the O Bar J could carry 150 cows, about ten per section. The O Bar J is now a small part of a cattle operation that grazes sixty-three sections where around 485 cows, fewer than eight cows per section, search for forage on the Sierrita bajada.

I cannot lay the blame on those who succeeded me, because the invasion by woody plants had begun long before Joe Miller said, "They're your cows now, John." But I must accept that my three years' use of the O Bar J range contributed to its deterioration, just as anyone, past or present, has done who has raised cattle in or on the fringes of the fragile, delicate desert grassland.

Perhaps we must accept that the desert grassland is a vegetation transition zone of the past. No man or woman alive can remember the true desert grassland. When the Spaniards came and Eusebio Francisco Kino brought livestock to his Pimería Alta, this delicate transition zone began to change. However, with the end of the grassland came the deterioration of a vast watershed, and the availability of water will limit human activity. Already the cities are claiming the water resources of the upper Santa Cruz Valley and elsewhere because urban Arizona has taken over the political power that the cowman once enjoyed. Que le vaya bien.

Index

About the Author

John Duncklee has pursued a varied life, working as a cowboy, sailor, university professor, mesquite furniture designer, and writer. He graduated from the University of Arizona in 1956 after a four-year hitch in the navy during the Korean War. After a number of years spent in cattle ranching, buying steers in Sonora, Mexico, farming near Tumacacori, consulting on the ranching business in Mexico, and breeding quarter horses on a ranch near Nogales, Arizona, he returned to the University of Arizona to attend graduate school in geography. He has taught at the University of Arizona, Northern Arizona University, and the Universidad de Sonora in Hermosillo.

While living in Flagstaff, Duncklee wrote the environmental impact statement *Man–Land Relationships on the San Francisco Peaks,* which was influential in halting an attempt to develop 160 acres of Hart Prairie on the western slope of the peaks. In conjunction with this effort, he wrote the lyrics and some of the music for the phonograph album *Did You Ever Sing to a Mountain.*

Since 1973 Duncklee has been a freelance writer and has had articles published in *Arizona Highways,* the *Christian Science Monitor, Defenders of Wildlife,* and the *Journal of Irreproducible Results.* His monthly column "View from the Porch" appears in the *Connection,* which is published in Arivaca, Arizona.